GOD WITH SKIN ON

*CYCLE C SERMONS FOR
ADVENT, CHRISTMAS, AND EPIPHANY
BASED ON THE GOSPEL TEXTS*

SUSAN R. ANDREWS

CSS PUBLISHING COMPANY, INC.
LIMA, OHIO

GOD WITH SKIN ON

FIRST EDITION
Copyright © 2015
by CSS Publishing Co., Inc.

Published by CSS Publishing Company, Inc., Lima, Ohio 45807. All rights reserved. No part of this publication may be reproduced in any manner whatsoever without the prior permission of the publisher, except in the case of brief quotations embodied in critical articles and reviews. Inquiries should be addressed to: CSS Publishing Company, Inc., Permissions Department, 5450 N. Dixie Highway, Lima, Ohio 45807.

Scripture quotations marked (NRSV) are from the New Revised Standard Version of the Bible. Copyright 1989 by the Division of Christian Education of the National Council of the Churches of Christ in the USA, Nashville, Thomas Nelson Publishers © 1989. Used by permission. All rights reserved.

Scripture quotations marked "The Message" are taken from The Message by Eugene H. Peterson, copyright © 1993, 1994, 1995, 1996, 2000, 2001, 2002. Used by permission of NavPress Publishing Group. All rights reserved.

Library of Congress Cataloging-in-Publication Data

Andrews, Susan R., 1949-
   God with skin on : Cycle C sermons for Advent, Christmas, and Epiphany based on the gospel texts / Susan R. Andrews. -- FIRST EDITION.
       pages cm
   ISBN 0-7880-2823-5 (alk. paper)
   1. Bible. Gospels--Sermons. 2. Sermons, American--21st century. 3. Advent sermons. 4. Christmas sermons. 5. Epiphany season--Sermons. 6. Church year sermons. 7. Common lectionary (1992). Year C. I. Title.

   BS2555.54.A53   2014
   252'.61--dc23

                                                    2014037542

For more information about CSS Publishing Company resources, visit our website at www.csspub.com, email us at csr@csspub.com, or call (800) 241-4056.

e-book:
ISBN-13: 978-0-7880-2824-3
ISBN-10: 0-7880-2824-3

ISBN-13: 978-0-7880-2823-6
ISBN-10: 0-7880-2823-5   PRINTED IN USA

*for my son, Nathan and my daughter, Anna
wonders of incarnation
in my life*

Other titles written by Susan R. Andrews:

Advent/Christmas/Epiphany section of
Sermons on the Gospel Readings, I, Cycle A
0-7880-2323-3 / $36.95

**The Tears of God:
Jesus as Passion and Promise**
Gospel Sermons for Lent/Easter, Cycle C
0-7880-2683-6 / $12.95

Other titles for Cycle C, Gospel Text
available through CSS are:

God With Skin On
Advent/Christmas/Epiphany
by Susan R. Andrews

Can I Get Some Help Over Here?
Lent/Easter
by R. Robert Cueni

Spirit Works
Pentecost Day through Proper 12
by Robert C. Cochran

Counting the Cost
Proper 13 through Proper 22
by George Reed, O.S.L.

Ordinary Gratitude
Proper 23 through Christ the King Sunday
by Molly F. James

Table of Contents

Preface — 7

Advent 1 — 9
    Crisis Management
    Luke 21:25-36

Advent 2 — 17
    Wilderness Work
    Luke 3:1-6

Advent 3 — 25
    Telling the Truth
    Luke 3:7-18

Advent 4 — 33
    The Future Present
    Luke 1:39-45 (46-55)

Christmas Eve / Day — 41
    God With Skin On
    Luke 2:1-14 (15-20)

Christmas 1 — 49
    Patterns of Possibility
    Luke 2:41-52

New Year's Day — 57
    Sheepish Shalom
    Matthew 25:31-46

Christmas 2 — 65
    Light Living
    John 1:(1-9) 10-18

Epiphany of Our Lord — 73
    How Intelligent Is God's Design?
    Matthew 2:1-12

Baptism of Our Lord — 83
  The Three Bs
  Luke 3:15-17, 21-22

Epiphany 2 — 91
  Is God Invited?
  John 2:1-11

Epiphany 3 — 99
  A Justice Jesus
  Luke 4:14-21

Epiphany 4 — 107
  How Angry Are You?
  Luke 4:21-30

Epiphany 5 — 115
  Trusting the Other Side
  Luke 5:1-11

Epiphany 6 — 123
  Holy Happiness
  Luke 6:17-26

Epiphany 7 — 131
  God's Absurd Answer
  Luke 6:27-38

Epiphany 8 — 139
  It's Not About Me
  Luke 6:39-49

Epiphany 9 — 147
  Trusting Authority
  Luke 7:1-10

Transfiguration of Our Lord — 155
  The Natural Look
  Luke 9:28-36 (37-43)

PREFACE

After forty years of ordained ministry, my faith has become simpler — and much more complex. Grace... gratitude... joy... justice... Jesus — the hundreds of sermons I have preached all boil down to a few, fierce fundamentals. And they all point to incarnation — the stunning realization that God is most present in the flesh. God-with-skin-on is the only God who can really touch us. The extraordinary power of God is most visible in the ordinary moments of living. If we cannot find God in this moment, in this place, we may not be able to find God at all.

Luke's gospel is the fleshiest of all the narratives of Jesus. There is more touch, taste, and tenderness in Luke than any of the other books in the New Testament. Luke has more healing stories, eating stories, children stories, birthing stories, and women stories than any of the other three gospels. And so in Year C, during Advent, Christmas, and Epiphany, we come face-to-face with our own human story. We become part of the incarnation — God becoming flesh in the daily-ness of our own living.

These sermons were preached in two very different settings. Most were delivered at Bradley Hills Presbyterian Church in Bethesda, a progressive growing congregation, where I served as Pastor/Head of Staff for seventeen years. The rest were preached within the 82 congregations of Hudson River Presbytery, where I have served as General Presbyter for the last eight years. As a result, some of these sermons are spoken to familiar friends, partners in vital ministry on a day-to-day basis. The rest are preached to relative strangers, struggling to be faithful disciples in the secular wilderness of the Northeast. And yet the message of incarnation is the same no matter where we preach it. God comes

— here — now — into every corner and crisis of our living — and wears the skin of our own humanity.
   This is the Good News of the gospel. May it be so!

Advent 1
Luke 21:25-36

"There will be signs in the sun, the moon, and the stars, and on the earth distress among nations confused by the roaring of the sea and the waves. People will faint from fear and foreboding of what is coming upon the world, for the powers of the heavens will be shaken. Then they will see 'the Son of Man coming in a cloud' with power and great glory. Now when these things begin to take place, stand up and raise your heads, because your redemption is drawing near." Then he told them a parable: "Look at the fig tree and all the trees; as soon as they sprout leaves you can see for yourselves and know that summer is already near. So also, when you see these things taking place, you know that the kingdom of God is near. Truly I tell you, this generation will not pass away until all things have taken place. Heaven and earth will pass away, but my words will not pass away. Be on guard so that your hearts are not weighed down with dissipation and drunkenness and the worries of this life, and that day catch you unexpectedly, like a trap. For it will come upon all who live on the face of the whole earth. Be alert at all times, praying that you may have the strength to escape all these things that will take place, and to stand before the Son of Man."

ADVENT 1
LUKE 21:25-36

CRISIS MANAGEMENT

It is a newspaper image I will never forget. And for me it is an image of Advent. The time was the early 1990s. The place was Sarajevo — the gutted, bombed out epicenter of the Balkan War — when ethnic violence had destroyed beauty and buildings and any sense of human community. One day, a man put on his tuxedo, picked up his cello and a chair, and went and sat at the central intersection of town — in the cross fire of hatred and brokenness and devastation — and there he played his cello for hours — defying all reason, embracing all hope — proclaiming through his melancholy melody that darkness and death never have the final word.

Today, my friends, is the first day of the Christian year, the beginning of Advent, the season of waiting where God is the darkness that promises light. Unlike the glare and noise and rush of the secular world — here within this sanctuary of our faith — we find ourselves in purple shadows — shadows of quiet and shadows of longing.

Advent is not a sub-category of Christmas. It is a time and a season unto itself. According to our liturgical calendar, Christmas doesn't begin until midnight on December 24. Before that miracle and that joy, however, comes four weeks of somber, sober, waiting and the brutally honest acknowledgment that the world is dark, our lives are dark, and the shadows we have created obscure God's light. Just when we're ready for a bit of good news, the scripture forces us to hear bad news. Just when we crave the comfort of a cradle in Bethlehem, our gospel text captures the gloomy predictions of an adult Jesus, spoken on his way to Jerusalem, on his way to the cross. You might well ask, "Why is the church so out of sync with the world? Why is the church confronting us with honest reality, when a bit of soft fantasy is what we long for?" Well, my friends, the answer is quite simple. It is the world that is out of sync with the church. It is the world that is out of sync with God.

The scripture readings for the First Sunday in Advent are always about the second coming. Not the first coming when Jesus embraces us with an infant's charm, but the second coming when the cosmic Christ assaults us with cataclysmic change. We read about strange signs in the sun and the moon, about stars falling from the sky, about a dark and frightening time when God will come in muscular form to wrestle with the forces of evil — a time so terrifying that people will faint from fear and foreboding. For the listeners of Luke's original words, these predictions spoke to the very heart of their existence — a time when Jerusalem had been destroyed, when the cruelty of Roman rule was suffocating the fledgling Christian community, and when staying faithful to God demanded courage amidst the seeming absence of God.

The problem is that these dire predictions of the imminent second coming did not happen as predicted. That does not mean that the crisis or the promise embedded in these predictions did not, does not, or will not come true. The central meaning of Advent is that God has a plan. God is present in the midst of apparent chaos. And no matter how deep our darkness, no matter how cataclysmic our crisis, God will continue to hold onto us — both with affection and with accountability.

So the question arises — where are the places this scripture speaks to us today — the places where the sun seems darkened in the lives of people we love — the places where all hell is breaking loose and cultural stars are falling hopelessly to the earth? You know the headlines as well as I do. After thousands of Iraqi and American lives were destroyed, Iraq is again doing a death dance inside a tinder box of suspicion and hatred. Generations continue to disappear in the violent and arid deserts of Africa. Here in the metropolitan New York area, despite the breathtaking rise of wealth, there has also been a 6% increase in those needing soup kitchens and food pantries. Millions of people continue to die from the devastation of AIDS — and most of the new victims are innocent women and children — twelve million children have been orphaned by AIDS in South Africa alone.

And the litany continues. In our diminished and conflicted denomination there are hyperbolic cries of constitutional crisis as we continue to struggle and vote about who is in and who is out within God's family of grace. In a statistical sense we mainline Protestants are in a big time crisis mode. Our denomination has lost 50% of its membership in the last fifty years. Here in the lower Hudson Valley, in the last fifteen years, our rolls have diminished 15%. Our worship attendance is down 15%, our mission giving is down 12%, and our infant baptisms are down 24%. One cynic has predicted that at the rate we are going, the last Presbyterian church will close its doors in 2085.

In many of your lives, there are personal crises — bitter marriages wounding and unraveling — bodies crippled by the relentless ravaging of cancer and disease — financial debts fed by the consumer seduction of our materialistic society and personal dreams shattered by the daily realities of boredom and responsibility. Yes, my friends, on this stark, dark New Year's Day of the Christian year, we are being called to recognize a world in crisis. We are called to acknowledge that we are not in control of the rhythms of life that can either make us hate God or cling to God as the only source of comfort and strength. Remember that in the Chinese language the symbol for crisis is twofold. It means both danger and opportunity. I wonder — what are the dangers and the opportunities of this Advent time in the life of the church, and in the lives of each one of us?

When I read the words of Luke 21 I see a simple outline of a particularly Christian course — a Christian Crisis Management Course: Crisis Management 101.

Crisis Management Step 1 — Look. See. Watch. "Heads up," Jesus says. Acknowledge the reality of the crisis. Look behind the gauzy curtain of Christmas nostalgia and see the pain. See the brokenness. See the despair. See the danger. Look for Herod — the Herod of modern day Hitler, the Herod of Assad, the Herod of TV evangelists preaching a gospel of prosperity and success instead of Jesus' gospel of service and compassion. Look for the despair of the homeless and the hungry, the lonely and the depressed — as well as the falling stars of our own lives — dreams that are deferred and relationships that are broken and values that are ignored — thus distancing us from the grace of God. Yes, Step 1 of Crisis Management is honesty.

Crisis Management Step 2 — Stay alert. Stay awake. Stay vigilant. Plan little. Expect anything. Accept everything. The uniqueness of our Christian God is that God is everywhere — in our human birthing, in our human grieving, in our human striving, in our human loving, in our human suffering, in our human dying. God is in the darkness and God is in the light. God is in the crisis and God is in the mystery. God is in the past and God is in the present. And God is absolutely, irrevocably, in the future.

My first boss was a senior pastor named Bill Barker. He was a complicated and faithful man who taught me much. I remember especially a late night conversation we had where, exhausted by the pendulum swings of a typical pastoral day, Bill shared with me how to manage the crises of a God-shaped life. Early that morning, Bill had been summoned to the bedside of a 101-year-old man who was dying. The two men prayed together and read scripture together. And then with the satisfaction of a life lived well, that 101-year-old disciple closed his eyes and died. It was the most stunning death Bill had ever witnessed. A crisis — which every death is — but a crisis of opportunity, managed with utter faithfulness.

Two hours later that same day, Bill officiated at the funeral service of a three-month-old baby who died of crib death. Wrenched apart by the pain of those young parents, Bill did the only thing he knew how to do. He uttered the promises of a God who is always with us, who never lets us go, who takes us through the darkest valleys of life until we find the promised light. One more crisis — the crisis of tragedy — this time managed with humble, honest hope.

Then late in the afternoon, Bill received a phone call from his son — announcing that Bill was a grandfather for the first time — that William P. Barker III had just fallen from heaven, a starburst of wonder streaking into a wounded world. A third crisis in one day — but this time the crisis of creation managed with the passion of love. Yes, for Bill Barker, that day was a whirlwind of crises — birth and death bumping up against one another — a day shaped by God's rhythms and God's reasons — and all Bill could do was stay alert, paying attention, expecting God to be God and opening up his own life as a channel of God's blessing.

This leads us to Crisis Management Step 3: Give up control and then take control. Yes, my friends, the best way to manage a crisis is to let God be God — intuitively trusting that everything depends on God — a God who tosses stars of life and death into our lap. Letting God be God also means to claim the God inside each of our souls. We must keep on working, keep on dreaming, keep on hoping, and keep on loving — just keep on keeping on — living as if everything depends on us. This is the paradox and the power and the promise of Advent. We are to watch as if everything depends on God. And then as we live between the beginning and the end of God's saving grace, we are to work as if everything depends on us.

    May it be so, for you and for me, in these uncertain times. Amen.

Advent 2
Luke 3:1-6

In the fifteenth year of the reign of Emperor Tiberius, when Pontius Pilate was governor of Judea, and Herod was ruler of Galilee, and his brother Philip ruler of the region of Ituraea and Trachonitis, and Lysanias ruler of Abilene, during the high priesthood of Annas and Caiaphas, the word of God came to John son of Zechariah in the wilderness. He went into all the region around the Jordan, proclaiming a baptism of repentance for the forgiveness of sins, as it is written in the book of the words of the prophet Isaiah, "The voice of one crying out in the wilderness: 'Prepare the way of the Lord, make his paths straight. Every valley shall be filled, and every mountain and hill shall be made low, and the crooked shall be made straight, and the rough ways made smooth; and all flesh shall see the salvation of God.' "

Advent 2
Luke 3:1-6

Wilderness Work

It was one of the most embarrassing moments of my life. I was sixteen, and it was my first game as the captain of the varsity cheerleading squad. Much to the dismay of the popular girls in the school, my loud voice had won me this hotly contested honor. The squad had been practicing all summer and we had our routines almost perfected. That early September night we were very excited and more than a bit nervous. The band picked up, the energy of the crowd erupted, and immediately the ball began to move rapidly down the field. With a shiver of anticipation, I cued the rest of the girls, and we started our cheer. *Touchdown, touchdown — we want a touchdown!* Voices screaming, arms pumping, legs jumping — it was exhilarating! Except that something was wrong. Our crowd was not responding but the one across the field was. I spun around to look at the field and almost fainted. Yes, the ball was moving down the field but in the wrong direction. You see, the other team had the ball and in my misguided enthusiasm, I had just cheered our rivals onto a touchdown.

Today, John the Baptist stands before us — bold, loud, energetic. Before he cheers us enthusiastically down the field, he asks us to check our spiritual compass — to check the direction of our lives. He implores us to make sure we know where we are headed. He asks us to make sure that we are clear about which direction we are carrying the message of our lives. And he assures us that it is not too late to repent

— to literally turn around. No, it's not too late to change the direction of our lives so that we won't miss the new life that God is promising to bring our way. We know that during this season of Advent, this season of new creation, we are called to wait and to watch and to expect but we are also called to participate in God's Advent. We are called to participate by preparing ourselves through repentance.

All four gospels force us to deal with bristly John the Baptist and always in early December, when the rest of the world is wrapped in soft, sweet celebration. John comes to us in the glare of biblical truth to confront us, to afflict us, to discomfort us, and to remind us that most of our preparations for Christmas don't prepare us for Christ at all. Luke's version of the John story begins in the immediacy of history. It begins right where we are, in the sixth year of Barack Obama's presidency, when Andrew Cuomo serves as governor of New York, and Nita Lowey sits in the House of Representatives, when Gradye Parsons serves as Stated Clerk of the Presbyterian Church, USA, and Heath Rada leads as the Moderator of the 221st General Assembly, in the year of our Lord 2015. The word of God comes to John — and through John, the word of God comes to us — to Cathy and Joan, to Bob and Joe, to Scott and to Lily — the word of God comes to us in the wilderness. Prepare a way for the Lord. Examine your life. Examine your priorities, your values, your behavior. Check out your emotional, your spiritual, and your ethical life. Are you headed in the right direction? Are you headed in the direction of the good? Are you headed in the direction of God? And if not, then repent, turn around, and change direction.

Are you unhealthy — your blood pressure too high, your cholesterol too rich, your weight too much? Repent — turn around. Change direction. How is your family life? Is it balanced, honest, open, and connected? Or is it stressed, precarious, lonely, brittle, or broken? Repent. Turn around. Change direction. What about your work — whether volunteer or paid — is your work rewarding, creative, compassionate — or is it tedious, overwhelming, demanding, and disconnected from your vision and your dreams, an unsatisfying use of your gifts and your energy? Repent. Turn around. Change direction. And what about your faith? Is it vital, growing, healing, and serving? Or is it small, tired, tepid, dull? Repent. Turn around. Change direction.

My friends, if we want God to come warmly, humanly, simply into our lives then we need to get ready. We need to prepare. We need to repent. We need to change. Yes, today John speaks uncomfortable words to us in a season where we yearn to be comfortable.

There is great tension these days within the Christian world about many things. But nothing is more troubling than the theological tension between grace and law, between acceptance and judgment, between God as lover and God as judge. Recently within the presbytery I serve, our gathered body passed an overture to the General Assembly calling for gun violence prevention. It grew out of a multi-congregational process of gun owners and gun control advocates struggling with what it means to be peacemakers in Christ's name. The overture focused on education and called for a ban on assault weapons and a limit on ammunition while also defending the second amendment right to own a gun. There was great joy and energy in the room when the overture passed with just one negative vote.

But a few days later, I received a well worded but angry letter from a woman in the presbytery who is a retired police officer. She had read the overture and felt that it did not adequately understand or honor the work of law enforcement officers or military personal. Indeed, as a faithful Presbyterian elder, she was feeling judged by the other members of the presbytery. She seemed to be pointing to a contradiction in our liberal, grace defined presbytery:

"If your theology is so inclusive, so based on the primacy of God's gracious and accepting love, why are you being exclusive and judgmental about those with whom you disagree?"

In other words, how can judgment and grace co-exist in the same place? It was — and it is — a very good question. It underlines the discomfort we all have with these John the Baptist stories. If God comes freely and graciously for all of us in the full humanity of Jesus. If God is born in us whether we deserve it or not — how come we have to do something in order to receive it? Why do we have to repent in order to be forgiven? How come we have to change in order to receive God? What right does John — or anyone — have to judge us, to criticize us, to assume that we aren't okay just the way we are?

The answer is that John shouldn't — and he doesn't. Today, the words of John the Baptist — words crying in the wilderness of our humanity — are not words of criticism. They are words of choice. John was not judging our worth. He was inviting our wholeness. He was not criticizing our past. He was offering our future. John was communicating the paradox of our faith — that the free and lavish grace of God makes no difference unless we are accountable. The unconditional love of God cannot find fertile soil unless we first uproot the weeds in the wilderness of our souls. God does not judge us. John does not judge us. *We* are not to judge each other.

But the truth of the gospel is that we must judge ourselves — we must face the truth of who we are and claim the hope of who we want to become. And after we judge ourselves — after we honor this call to accountability — then we can receive God, as God recreates us in holy image. This is the work of Advent. This is the work of preparation. This is the work of repentance. This is the work of turning around to face the direction of God. And the result? Exquisite freedom and abundant life!

There is a medieval legend, adapted from a story told by Thomas Troeger, about a man who was decadent and irresponsible in many ways but who had enough grace in him to want to be good. He went to a costume maker who gave him a costume to wear — complete with a halo wired to his head. As the man walked down the street he was tempted to act in his normal, shiftless way. Then he remembered the halo on his head and he decided to act differently. He gave money to a beggar on the street. He treated his wife well. He refused to cut corners at work. Eventually he returned the halo costume but as he was leaving the costume shop he caught a glimpse of himself in the mirror and he saw a permanent halo glowing above his head! It seems that he had become what he did — that his repentance had made possible God's forgiveness and transformation in his life. Yes, by turning around and beginning to behave in a new way this man found a permanent new direction for his life.

My friends, through our baptism we receive a halo that is permanently attached to our soul, but we need to be about the business of looking in the mirror of our days and polishing that halo with repentance and intent. John makes it clear this morning that repentance is what we do so that God will have space and a place to make us into new people — so that God can complete the baptismal blessing of our lives.

Somehow when I think of Advent, of repentance, of preparation, I don't have visions of arid deserts and wild prophets. I think instead of the wide open fields of North Dakota and Minnesota — with acres of sunflowers turning their faces toward the sun. The beauty of these flowers is in their responsive turn. Their health and wholeness comes from their openness to the sun. Their life is defined by what the light can give them. So it is for us in the fields of our daily living. My friends, let us turn around and turn our faces toward the light of the world and let us shine.

May it be so for you and for me. Amen.

Advent 3
Luke 3:7-18

John said to the crowds that came out to be baptized by him, "You brood of vipers! Who warned you to flee from the wrath to come? Bear fruits worthy of repentance. Do not begin to say to yourselves, 'We have Abraham as our ancestor'; for I tell you, God is able from these stones to raise up children to Abraham. Even now the ax is lying at the root of the trees; every tree therefore that does not bear good fruit is cut down and thrown into the fire." And the crowds asked him, "What then should we do?" In reply he said to them, "Whoever has two coats must share with anyone who has none; and whoever has food must do likewise." Even tax collectors came to be baptized, and they asked him, "Teacher, what should we do?" He said to them, "Collect no more than the amount prescribed for you." Soldiers also asked him, "And we, what should we do?" He said to them, "Do not extort money from anyone by threats or false accusation, and be satisfied with your wages." As the people were filled with expectation, and all were questioning in their hearts concerning John, whether he might be the Messiah, John answered all of them by saying, "I baptize you with water; but one who is more powerful than I is coming; I am not worthy to untie the thong of his sandals. He will baptize you with the Holy Spirit and fire. His winnowing fork is in his hand, to clear his threshing floor and to gather the wheat into his granary; but the chaff he will burn with unquenchable fire." So, with many other exhortations, he proclaimed the good news to the people.

Advent 3
Luke 3:7-18

Telling the Truth

Of the four gospel accounts in the New Testament, Luke is my favorite. Luke is warm and simple, full of love and joy, healing and grace. And Luke treats women better than any other book in the Bible. It is in Luke that we find the beloved Christmas story — with baby sighs and soft skin and angel wings. Then we get to Luke's third chapter and the tone shifts. Warm, fuzzy Jesus is abruptly replaced by loud, livid John. And we learn that even Luke's good news is often proclaimed in a bad news world. Even Luke finds it necessary to remind us that the gospel message is not a fairy tale about bouncing babies and radiant rainbows. The good news is a reality show and it begins amidst the shards of our broken lives. The good news begins by telling the truth.

I find John's truth-telling refreshing and cathartic. Telling the truth out loud — to each other — feels like a refining fire of freedom. Telling the truth brings us to our knees in supplication and need, preparing us to submit body and soul to the fresh gift of love and grace that only God can provide.

This day let us hear John the Baptist talking to us. Repent! Confess. Prepare a highway in the desert of your broken promises and your broken dreams.

Harold Kurtz was an old man with a young heart. He was an evangelical Christian, but in the best sense of that world, because, you see, "evangelical" comes from the Greek that literally means *good news* — and Harold Kurtz was a good news kind of guy. For almost forty years he was a missionary in Ethiopia passionately sharing Jesus with hungry people — people hungry for food — people hungry for God. But long before he was a missionary he was a bomber pilot in WWII — one of five sons in his family to go to war.

In the early 2000s, toward the end of his life, Harold wrote a passionate editorial calling us as a nation to repent. He wrote:

> *Lately I feel like a stranger in the United States. I am a remnant of what has been called "the greatest generation," but it's not the thinning ranks of my generation that has me feeling lost and confused. It's the debate about torture that has been swirling around me for months. I never imagined such a debate in my country.*

Then Harold described how, during the WWII, he would drop supplies to the enemy troops as well as his own, how both American and Germans soldiers would lay side by side as he ferried the wounded to field hospitals, how after he helped capture POWs inside enemy territory, the Americans shared their limited K-rations with foe as well as friend. At the same time, back home, in Oregon, his mom and dad were trying to eke out a living on their family farm without the help of their boys who were fighting overseas. There was a German POW camp close to the farm and Harold's parents began to use some of the enemy prisoners to help them till the soil. Harold's mom couldn't stand to see how thin those soldiers were, so she started cooking stews and nourishing soups and inviting them into the kitchen where they ate, sang, and prayed together. Harold concluded:

> *I am an evangelical Christian. Jesus tells us to eliminate our enemies by making friends of them. I am certain all of those prisoners who worked on our farm went back to*

Germany not as enemies but as friends. What has happened to my country? How can my country be debating the merits of torture? [Or unannounced drone attacks?] Why has my country lost the will to make friends out of enemies? What we need is a "single statement from the executive branch of our government that torture is forbidden everyplace, all the time, by every agency and under all circumstances..."[1]

John the Baptist said: Repent. Confess. Prepare a highway in the desert of your broken promises and your broken dreams.

Despite my moral resolve to simplify Christmas, I have already bought more doodads and trinkets than anybody needs or wants. The headline story on the evening news was the glad giddy tidings that Black Friday was a triumph — on the day after Thanksgiving we Americans grabbed more goodies in the mall than last year. With the stock market again rising and inflation remaining low, our economy is once again getting stronger. But my friends, let's tell the truth. The economy is strong primarily for us, for the rich, for the beneficiaries of a gluttonous tax policy, while at the same time, the bankruptcy rate has skyrocketed and foreclosures are still devastating families. While the number of hungry children and deported immigrant children in America has risen, while hundreds and thousands of the invisible poor are dying in the deserts of Africa, decaying in the ghettoes of America, and disappearing in the refugee camps of Syria and Lebanon, our economy shows improvement.

John the Baptist said: Repent. Confess. Prepare a highway in the desert of your broken promises and your broken dreams.

I continue to cringe at each story recounting the number of people executed in the United States since the death penalty, over 1,350, since it was re-instituted in the 1980s. I was impressed to learn that the European Union has totally banned the death penalty. And I was horrified to learn that the four nations with the highest death penalty numbers in the world are China, Iran, Vietnam and yes, the good old US of A. What kind of brutal, totalitarian company are we keeping?

John the Baptist said: Repent. Confess. Prepare a highway in the desert of your broken promises and your broken dreams.

But lest we think that John is only concerned about the sins of the political world, about the sins of all those bad politicians and leaders out there, let's bring all of this in here — into your life and mine. When I pull my own sins into the light of day, it is not a pretty picture. The cynicism of my mid-life years, the judgment and pettiness toward family, friends, and coworkers is not pretty. My irresponsibility in terms of over-working, over-eating, over-drinking, and over-worrying is not pretty. My sense of hopelessness when I look at the state of the Christian church and the state of the world and the state of my own tired heart is not pretty either.

John the Baptist said: Repent. Confess. Prepare a highway in the desert of your broken promises and your broken dreams.

By now, I imagine that some of you are muttering to yourselves — enough already. It's Christmas, for God's sake! Stop this relentless mantra of judgment and sin, this depressing litany of doom and gloom. But my friends that is what we always say when we are confronted by prophets, when we are confronted by the truth. And in scripture, the prophets — Elijah and Amos and Jeremiah and Ezekiel and Jesus — the prophets are ostracized and criticized and yes, even killed. Except that today, in the gospel message, a strange thing happens. Today, we are told that people from all over Judea — crowds of people — are thronging to hear the prophet. Yes, they are eagerly gathering to be bombarded by the truth. Why? Because they sense that in the midst of the Baptist's blast there is also the blessed truth — the good news that with God, and in God, and only by God, all things can be new. In Luke that good news is clear — a new reality is about to happen, and we can be part of it. But only if we change our lives, open our hearts, and worry about other people more than we worry about ourselves.

We often think of the Old Testament as discomforting and the New Testament as comforting. But this morning all of that is reversed. There are no more comforting words than the vision in chapter 40 of Isaiah. The first 39 books of Isaiah are all about telling the truth — about the reality of Israel's sin — about the failing, flailing people who have been dragged into exile because of their broken promises and their broken dreams. Then in a stunning reversal, chapter 40 turns everything around. The people are still failing, still flailing in the arid desert of exile, but God, through the prophet, transforms judgment into joy.

"Comfort my people," God says to Isaiah. "Speak tenderly to them. Proclaim that the glory of the Lord has come, that the glory of the Lord is coming, that the glory of the Lord will come again. Tell my people that the penalty has already been paid, and that the rough plains will be smoothed out, and the low places shall be brought high. Announce that the might of the Lord will bring healing to the broken world and that the mercy of the Lord will pick up Israel — like a shepherd carrying a lamb. I the Lord God will pick up Israel and carry her home. Yes, Isaiah, because you have spoken the truth, because the people have confessed the truth, because all of you are the still the treasure of my heart, because of all these things, I the Lord *will* make everything new."

My friends, these are the words and this is the memory that John evokes today as he proclaims repentance and transformation. Yes, John is announcing that the glad tidings first imagined by Isaiah have now become real. They are and will be incarnated, embodied in a person and in a way through which all of us can start over and become fresh, forgiven, and free.

The church I served years ago in New Jersey was a small, blue collar congregation that worshiped in a white clapboard building — a tiny sanctuary that could seat no more than a hundred people. There was only one stained glass window in that spartan space — a somewhat primitive window, in the back, made out of cheap glass. But the image in that window was priceless. It was the image of Jesus, the good shepherd, gathering the lambs in his arms, gently carrying them — gently carrying us — in his bosom. Every week as I stared at that window I felt cherished and safe.

My friends, this promise is still the good news — good news with no strings attached. But you know and I know that we cannot truly hear this good news until we first confess the bad news — until we tell the whole truth and nothing but the truth about the brokenness and the deep need of our lives.

Repent. Confess. Prepare a highway in the desert of your broken promises and your broken dreams. This is the beginning of the Good News of Jesus Christ. Hear it. Trust it. Practice it. And then wait for God to pick you up and tenderly carry you home.

May it be so for you and for me. Amen.

---

1. Source unknown.

Advent 4
Luke 1:39-45 (46-55)

In those days Mary set out and went with haste to a Judean town in the hill country, where she entered the house of Zechariah and greeted Elizabeth. When Elizabeth heard Mary's greeting, the child leaped in her womb. And Elizabeth was filled with the Holy Spirit and exclaimed with a loud cry, "Blessed are you among women, and blessed is the fruit of your womb. And why has this happened to me, that the mother of my Lord comes to me? For as soon as I heard the sound of your greeting, the child in my womb leaped for joy. And blessed is she who believed that there would be a fulfillment of what was spoken to her by the Lord."

ADVENT 4
LUKE 1:39-45 (46-55)

THE FUTURE PRESENT

We Protestants don't know what to do with Mary. Because the doctrines of the Catholic church have turned Mary into a sweet passive icon of virginal purity, we Protestants have been content to leave her out of our gallery of biblical saints — except of course, for her obligatory appearance in our Christmas pageants.

Today in both scripture and song, we meet Mary again. The woman we meet this time is no quiescent vessel. Lifting up the radical reversals of God's vision, this Mary predicts a revolution — the revolution that Jesus' life and message will bring to the world. She reminds us that what will be — already is. The future is already present because God is in charge of the world. We have a choice. We can either get with the program and help God complete this revolution, or we will find ourselves scattered and sent empty away.

Mary's passionate song of praise is rooted in the Hebrew scriptures. It echoes the main theme of Hannah's song of praise — uttered by an old barren woman who has finally been blessed with fruitfulness of body and soul. And like Hannah, Mary is overwhelmed by the generosity of a graceful God who intentionally picks those who are lowly — barren women, teenage peasants, invisible people — ordinary sinners like you and me — yes, God picks us to do, and be, and bear good news for the world.

My daughter Anna works as a ninth grade English teacher in an inner city, all black high school in St. Louis. One of the challenges of her job has been to move beyond — to move behind — the images of mouthy, scary, black street kids that most of us suburbanites have created in our minds and hearts. Anna has learned that, indeed, urban teens *are* mouthy, but in a delightfully creative and energetic way. She has learned that the lack of discipline or achievement in many of their lives is a burden for them, as well as for the larger culture.

Like Mary, some of Anna's fourteen-year-old girls are poor and pregnant outside of wedlock. As a result, they are stigmatized and rejected by the "proper" world. Anna sees one of her tasks as helping these teenage girls see their lives as possibilities and as channels of God's grace. It's too bad that in a public school Anna cannot have her girls read today's text — for it is God's emphatic promise that in the economy of God's grace, the poor will be lifted up and the hungry will be filled with good things.

Mary's song of praise is intended to be good news. It is the good news that the child she is bearing is the fulfillment of God's dream and plan for the world — the good news that what God hopes for is already present in the very imagination of creation. And her God, our God, will not rest until this imagined realm of peace and justice and abundance and joy and hope *for all* is fully realized.

But, wait a minute, we might ask, though this vision of God is good news for the poor, for those who will be lifted up and filled with good things. How can this vision be good news for us — for those of us who, in comparison, are the proud and the rich that Mary's song describes? The message seems pretty clear — the proud and the self-sufficient are scattered and the affluent and the successful are sent empty away. This is good news?

Absolutely! Because my friends, when we become proud and puffed up and full of ourselves and our accomplishments and our importance, there comes a point when we have no more room for God. And when we get too rich, when we get distracted by too many things and too many agendas and too much money, we begin to feel that God is no longer necessary — and we cut ourselves off from what really matters, what really fills our souls, what only comes from a full measure of God's Spirit in our lives. What *really* matters is love, grace, worship, relationships, and joyful service in the world.

I think in my life, I get the "rich" part — the fact that because we are, relatively speaking, part of the 2% of richest folk in the world, it is our responsibility and our privilege to share that wealth extravagantly and sacrificially with those who have little. And the generosity of many congregations — especially for designated opportunities, disaster relief, special Christmas offerings — shows that we understand that giving generously not only helps the world, but makes us feel better. The good news is that the great economic reversal described in Mary's revolutionary song, doesn't do to the rich what the rich have been doing to the poor since the beginning of time. It doesn't make them (us) poor. Instead it turns an ethic of scarcity for some and competition among all into an ethic of generosity, where everyone has what they need.

The part of this text about the rich, I get. But it is the proud part that I have been forced to learn. Serving as moderator of the PCUSA for a year was a thrilling and invigorating experience. But it was also, in some ways, very bad for my soul. You know, without even realizing it is happening, it can go to your head when people stand every time you enter a room — the custom for honoring the role of the moderator in our denomination. It can puff up a soul when people wine and dine you and say extravagant things about you all over the country and all around the world. And so for me, coming back down to earth, resuming the quotidian, repetitive duties of parish ministry — returning to a wonderful place where my weaknesses as well as my strengths are named, and I am reminded often that I am very, very human — all of this has been difficult, but very healing. Thank God that God has taken my pride and with gentle judgment, scattered it, so that I can reclaim the modesty and the ministry that is the real calling in my life.

My friends, when Mary sings her revolutionary song this morning, she is singing good news for all of us — rich and poor, proud and humble, ancient and modern. The life abundant in spirit and love is an abundance that all people in all times and places are called to create and to enjoy. But the main point of Mary's melody is not to focus on us, but to focus on God. "My soul magnifies the Lord," she sings. In other words, my soul, my life is a magnifying glass enlarging God. The blessings of my life are not about me — but about the one who blesses all of creation with hope and meaning.

We are left this morning with the purpose of the Christian life — a purpose defined by this model of discipleship named Mary. The purpose of our Christian lives is to bear the image of God within our very bodies, within our very souls. And when the Spirit of God fills us to the brim with blessings there simply is no longer room for the pride or the wealth that has distracted us in the past. It is then that we can magnify, that we can enlarge God's presence for all the world to see.

At Bible study we heard the story of Miriam Smith, who was a Sunday school teacher at the Bethesda Presbyterian Church in the early 1950s. One of the mantras of Mrs. Smith's Bible lessons was instructive not just to the children but to the adults as well. She said that when we allow our lives to magnify God, we automatically become small in comparison — not small in a poor-me sense, but small in a divine/human sense. In that smallness we can fit into that one unique spot each one of us has in this intricate puzzle called life — that one unique spot that only we can fill in God's magnificent vision of peace and joy.

My friends, on this Rejoice Sunday in the season of Advent, let us commit ourselves to magnify God — to enlarge God — through the small, utterly unique gift of our irreplaceable lives.

May it be so for you and for me. Amen.

Christmas Eve / Day
Luke 2:1-14 (15-20)

In those days a decree went out from Emperor Augustus that all the world should be registered. This was the first registration and was taken while Quirinius was governor of Syria. All went to their own towns to be registered. Joseph also went from the town of Nazareth in Galilee to Judea, to the city of David called Bethlehem, because he was descended from the house and family of David. He went to be registered with Mary, to whom he was engaged and who was expecting a child. While they were there, the time came for her to deliver her child. And she gave birth to her firstborn son and wrapped him in bands of cloth, and laid him in a manger, because there was no place for them in the inn. In that region there were shepherds living in the fields, keeping watch over their flock by night. Then an angel of the Lord stood before them, and the glory of the Lord shone around them, and they were terrified. But the angel said to them, "Do not be afraid; for see — I am bringing you good news of great joy for all the people: to you is born this day in the city of David a Savior, who is the Messiah, the Lord. This will be a sign for you: you will find a child wrapped in bands of cloth and lying in a manger." And suddenly there was with the angel a multitude of the heavenly host, praising God and saying, "Glory to God in the highest heaven, and on earth peace among those whom he favors!"

Christmas Eve / Day
Luke 2:1-14 (15-20)

God With Skin On

As we gather here this holy night, we come from a variety of religious backgrounds. For some of you I'm sure the more familiar word during The Lord's Prayer is "trespasses." You will especially appreciate an internet story about the little boy who was sent to bed early on Christmas Eve. His boisterous excitement was getting in the way of all the hectic, last minute preparations his parents were trying to make, and they needed to get rid of him. A few minutes later his father overheard the child saying his prayers by the side of his bed — a bit confused, but poignant nonetheless. "And God," the child said, "please forgive us our Christmases as we forgive those who Christmas against us."

Christmas can be so wonderful. And it can be so terrible as we get caught up in the whirlwind — trying to doing it all. We get caught up trying to imitate Grandma and trying to balance the true meaning of this night with the TV inspired expectations of our children. As the poet W.H. Auden suggested, we are so materially bound, that we fail to see "the actual vision," and only find fleeting time to entertain it as "an agreeable possibility." We gather here tonight — some of us content, happy, relaxed — but all too many of us tired, stressed, guilty, anxious. Yes, we come here tonight restless, because despite all our preparation, we still don't know what we are preparing for — why it is that in the deepest part of who we are, there is an emptiness and a hunger.

We come to church, some of us settled in familiar pews, others of us feeling a bit awkward because this is foreign territory and we're not quite sure how to do all those things listed in the bulletin. But all of us are like the soldier during World War II who had his face blown apart, causing both disfigurement and amnesia. He didn't know who he was or where he belonged. He began to visit villages, trying to find himself. After several tries he stepped off the train onto a particular main street and "something about the station and its environment seemed familiar. As he walked down the street, it all began to come back, and he turned this way and that, growing increasingly more sure of where he was, until he arrived at the cottage where his family lived and knew that he was home."[1]

My friends, tonight we have come home. It's all beginning to feel familiar — the sweet voices in the darkness, the comfort of well sung carols, the anticipation of light spreading warmth in our midst, and those words about a place and time when God was real. It is a place and a time that can become real again tonight. It is a simple Palestinian village where a husband and a wife weep and laugh over a baby — a soft, fragrant baby who looks up at us with total trust and innocence, waiting for us to take care of him. Grimy shepherds, terrified and electrified by an army of angels lighting up the sky with the transcendent glory of the same God who lies helpless in the manger. How odd and how wonderful! Yes, caught up by the familiarity, we are drawn into the story. And maybe if we let go and sink into it, we can touch, taste, see, hear, and smell this story. Maybe — for a minute — that emptiness deep inside of us can be filled by a very real, very living, very loving God. Maybe the agreeable possibility can become the actual vision — where everything is *you* and nothing is *it*.

A Canadian pastor tells the true story about a little girl who was being put to bed by her mother during a loud thunderstorm. As the mother tried to leave, the little girl insisted that she stay to comfort her during the storm. The mother explained that she and Daddy wanted to eat dinner and spend some time together. The mother tried to calm the little girl by saying, "God will take care of you. There's no need to be afraid." The little girl cried out, "I know Mommy, but when it thunders that way, a little girl like me wants somebody with skin on!"[2]

After all the theological arguments and philosophical debates, after all the careful exegesis of biblical minutiae, what Christmas boils down to is this — God with skin on — a God who wants to be loved and not feared, a God who chooses to become particular and personal with us where we are, a God who becomes human in order to teach us and invite us to become divine. The great divide — the divine/human gap — becomes instead, this night, an intimate relationship between partners in creation. That which is common becomes holy — and we need never be lonely again — we need never be scared again — we certainly will never be the same again.

My family and I were fortunate enough to get tickets to the Vermeer exhibit at the National Gallery of Art — the most complete showing of the artist's work ever to be assembled. A deeply religious man, Vermeer expressed his faith through his work. But there is nothing "religious" about this art. His portraits are small and limited in subject matter — common people in common places doing common things. And yet to see these paintings and to be embraced by them is a holy experience. It is the light and the skin that does it — soft, moist, luminous skin that begs to be touched and kissed and caressed — common human flesh that glows with the full-bodied spirit of the divine: incarnation — God with us. In these human-holy portraits, Vermeer proclaims the reality of God in the midst of the artist's everyday human experience.

When the angels startled the somnolent shepherds in those grimy fields outside Bethlehem — the angels proclaimed: "This shall be the sign for you. You will find a baby wrapped in swaddling cloths and lying in a manger." The shepherds left immediately to find this sign and they were so excited about this God-thing breaking into their very human existence that they become irresponsible. They did not follow the process, they did not do their duty, they did not meet management objectives. They left the sheep unattended and went to see this thing that had happened.

And indeed they found a baby wrapped in swaddling cloths and lying in a manger. This year I have become fascinated with this image of swaddling cloth — mentioned twice by Luke — and only three other times in scripture. A swaddling cloth was a large square cloth with a long diagonal strip hanging off one corner. The baby was wrapped in the cloth and then the long strip was wound firmly around the full length of the infant — for warmth, for security, to remind the child of the dark, safe, protection of the womb. Just in the past year, as I have held my swaddled grandson in my arms, I have been reminded all over again about how important warm, snug love can be for a newborn baby. In Hebrew scripture whenever this word *swaddling* appears, it refers to a child who is beloved, who is special, and who is safe amidst the terror of real life. And so it is with Jesus — with *Yeshua* — whose Hebrew name means salvation. This beloved child, safe amidst the terror of a Herod-filled world, is swaddled salvation, tightly wrapped wholeness. This child is God's promise — tangible and visible — God with skin on.

Can you see the baby? Reach out and touch him. You are touching God — safe, precious, special, beloved. But look again. You are also touching yourself. For you too are safe, precious, special, beloved. Through your baptism you have become one with Christ and you have become a bit of God with skin on. There are swaddling cloths of grace wrapped tightly around you. Can you feel them? They are there to keep you safe, to keep you warm, and to tell you just how beloved you are. But then, please look in the manger one more time. What you see is not just God — or yourself. What you see are all the brothers and sisters around you — all the people for whom salvation has come — safe, precious, special, beloved. You see those for whom God sent Jesus, because God so loved the world. And if we can see the multicolored face of humanity in the baby — with all the physical and spiritual needs that come with innocent human life — then we will also see and hear our calling. For when this God with skin on gets under our skin, our calling is to wrap all of God's precious children with swaddling cloths of protection and love.

George was the custodian of a small church in rural Louisiana. He was married to Alice and together they had six children. One afternoon, Alice, aged 34, was hanging wash in the backyard and dropped dead of a heart attack. One of the church elders who was a friend, upon hearing of the death, went to be with George. When he arrived George was stretched out on the bed staring at the ceiling, numb. His friend said nothing, but instead pulled up a rocker and sat down by the bed. He lit up a cigar and began to rock. George drifted into soul-soothing sleep as night fell. Later George recounted how on the day Alice died he awoke in the dark and instinctively reached out for Alice, but she was not there. When he touched the empty side of the bed, he was stabbed awake by the agony of his lostness and loneliness. Just as the pain of isolation became unbearable, George said he caught in the corner of his eye an arcing red glow, the movement of his friend's lit cigar as he rocked quietly. "I got through the night because my friend was *there*."[3]

Brothers and sisters, we can get through this night and all the dark nights of the soul, because God is there — because God is here — swaddling us with grace that holds us tight and keeps us safe — so that we can become the presence of God for others. Our God is a God with skin on — in all the people and all the experiences and all the intuitions — that lead us to a place of peace and wholeness.

May it be so, for you and for me. Amen.

---

1. John Killinger, *Lectionary Homiletics*, December 1992, p. 25.

2. Leonard A. Griffith, *Lectionary Homiletics*, December 1989, p. 36, adapted.

3. Don Wardlaw, *Lectionary Homiletics*, January 1992, p. 9, adapted.

Christmas 1
Luke 2:41-52

Now every year his parents went to Jerusalem for the festival of the Passover. And when he was twelve years old, they went up as usual for the festival. When the festival was ended and they started to return, the boy Jesus stayed behind in Jerusalem, but his parents did not know it. Assuming that he was in the group of travelers, they went a day's journey. Then they started to look for him among their relatives and friends. When they did not find him, they returned to Jerusalem to search for him. After three days they found him in the temple, sitting among the teachers, listening to them and asking them questions. And all who heard him were amazed at his understanding and his answers. When his parents saw him they were astonished; and his mother said to him, "Child, why have you treated us like this? Look, your father and I have been searching for you in great anxiety." He said to them, "Why were you searching for me? Did you not know that I must be in my Father's house?" But they did not understand what he said to them. Then he went down with them and came to Nazareth, and was obedient to them. His mother treasured all these things in her heart. And Jesus increased in wisdom and in years, and in divine and human favor.

Christmas 1
Luke 2:41-52

Patterns of Possibility

A few years ago I revisited the places of my childhood. Sim and I piled the kids into the car and traveled to LaCrosse, Wisconsin, where I was born, and then to Erie, Pennsylvania, where I lived from the age of five until the age of twelve. Together the four of us explored what Sim fondly called the Seven Sacred Susie Sightings: the house where I was born, the two elementary schools I attended, the park by the zoo where I flew up from Brownie Scouts to Girl Scouts, and the beach on Lake Erie where I spent hour after lazy hour floating in the warmth of summer. We also visited the two churches, in Erie and LaCrosse, where my father had served as pastor, and where I had lived, happily, for many, many years. I say "lived" purposely — for those two church buildings became, for me, like second homes. Not only did the pews feel as familiar as my living room sofa, the tunnels under the church building, the closet behind the balcony, the classrooms in the Sunday school assembly hall — all these spaces became familiar places to hide in and play in and grow in.

But when Sim and the kids and I first drove up to the red brick church building in scenic downtown Erie, I didn't recognize the facade. Years ago the First Presbyterian Church had been sold to Gannon College, and the sanctuary had been transformed into a Catholic college chapel — complete with statues of the Virgin Mary and holy water at the main entrances to the sanctuary. At first I was angry and disappointed. But then, when I went in and sat down, it all came flooding back to me — the complete safety and familiarity I have always felt in the church — and I knew that at some level, I had come home.

These experiences which shaped my childhood give me an entree into today's gospel story that may be different from yours. Jesus' behavior in this wonderful tale has never particularly bothered me or surprised me. Actually, it makes total sense to me that Jesus would stay behind in the temple, comfortable with the space and the priests and the holiness of the sanctuary. Why not? He had been raised by faithful parents who took him regularly to his hometown synagogue, and who had brought him here, to the special temple in Jerusalem, every single year of his life. You see this is what practicing Jewish parents were expected to do. From the moment of circumcision at the prescribed eight days, to dedication at six weeks, to the yearly sojourns for prayer and sacrifice, to this special occasion on his twelfth birthday, Jesus had been brought to the temple in Jerusalem and swept up in the rhythms and rituals of the Jewish faith. For him, to be in the temple felt like a warm bath, a sacred home, and a place of total acceptance and exciting challenge.

Mary and Joseph had taught Jesus that he did not belong to them — that he belonged to God — that he had only been lent to them for a few years. Jesus understood that his world was bigger than Nazareth. He understood that God's family was bigger than Mary, Joseph, and his brothers and sisters. He understood that God's table was bigger than his kitchen table. And he understood that his life, his identity, his purpose was bigger than being the oldest son of Joe and Mary. Yes, without even realizing it, these are lessons that Mary and Joseph passed onto their boy. Ironically, Jesus understood and accepted these lessons much better than did the two people who taught him.

I've always known, in my head, that the purpose of being a parent is to let our children go. I've always known in my head that the only reason we hug them tight is so that they will feel secure when they flee our arms to embrace the world. But when the idea begins to become reality, it doesn't always feel very good.

Maxie Dunham tells simple pithy stories that capture the wisdom of ordinary living. In one such story he recounts the day a young man left home for college. His mother had helped him pack and then drove him to his new dormitory. After a warm hug, she quickly and quietly left him to get settled on his own. As he was unpacking his suitcase, he found his shirts and pants and underwear all carefully stacked. And tucked in with them were two long narrow strips of cloth, neatly ironed and folded. He had no idea what they were at first. But then looking at them closely, he recognized their pattern. These were the strings from his mother's apron. And she had cut them off — in order to set him free. In my own journey with my young adult children, I cannot tell you how many times I have reminded myself of the wisdom of this simple story. Many times I have once again symbolically cut off the spiritual apron strings I am unconsciously using to control their lives.

Jesus began to separate from his parents, so that he could become closer to the God buried deep within his own soul. But his actions caused some to raise their eyebrows over the years. In fact, some interpreters have accused Jesus of being anti-family. This morning he seems astonished by the acute anxiety of his two over-protective parents. His response was less than respectful. Who *are* these crazy people? he thought. So we've been apart for five days. What's the big deal? Don't they trust me enough to know that I will eventually come home? After all *they* are the ones who made me comfortable with the priest, who introduced me to this temple and to these scriptures that fascinate me so.

But today's episode was only the beginning of Jesus' strange relationship with his family. Years later, when he arrived back in Nazareth to preach his first sermon, he embarrassed mom and dad by preaching not a warm safe message to impress the neighbors, but a prophetic, scary message, that made everyone mad. Then, at his first miracle — you know, where he changed water into wine at a cousin's wedding — Jesus sharply rebuked Mary in front of the entire family. And a few weeks later when his mother and brothers came to get him at the synagogue trying to convince him to rest — Jesus turned on them and said: "Who are my mother, my brothers, my family? Not you. Oh, no. My family is everyone who hears the word of God and does it." At the bitter end, when he was hanging on the cross, and his mother was weeping at his feet, Jesus gently pushed his mother away — giving her a new family — saying to Mary: "Mother, behold your new son." And to John: "Son, behold your new mother."

Actually, my friends, Jesus was not anti-family. He just defined family in a new way — in a much bigger and broader way. We are all brothers and sisters to each other. We are all called to nurture and to need a large group of people in order to become whole. In fact, when we focus exclusively or obsessively on the few people with whom we share a house, we risk turning "family" into an idol and we end up avoiding the larger responsibilities of kinship that God has called us to embrace.

At first glance, today's story is about parents and children, about adolescence, and about the wider perspective and context that a disciplined spiritual life gives to our offspring and to us. But in a bigger sense, this gospel story is about a larger pattern of possibility that God has implanted in each of our souls. Whenever we decide that we have finally arrived, whenever we decide that we are finally established, whenever we decide that we are finished, or that we have life all figured out — yes, whenever we feel like we are settled — it is then that God surprises us with another whole chapter of living, whether we want it or not. At these points, we have a choice. We can either greet this surprise with anxiety and anger, as did Mary and Joseph, or we can welcome the surprise with curiosity and openness, as did Jesus. You see, the frontiers of identity formation are not just an adolescent phenomenon. Becoming who we are is a perpetual process, a continual blessing, because we are the ever-unfolding children of God. But — and this is important — trust and not control is the only way we can unfold without collapsing.

Years ago, when I served a large congregation in Pennsylvania, there was a prominent family who was ever-present in the workings of the church. John, the father, was a benevolent patriarch — very wealthy, very demanding, and very authoritative. His children did what he said — including active involvement in all aspects of the church. As a young associate pastor, I worked with the youth and young adults in that congregation, including the daughters of this family. A strange thing happened on their journey toward adulthood. All three of his children ended up going to seminary — two of them eventually becoming parish pastors.

A few years later I remember having a conversation with John — who was simply mystified as to why his children would want to enter a profession with so little status and so little financial reward. I smiled, and then gently reminded him that he had presented his three children for baptism within the walls of the church — just as Mary and Joseph had presented Jesus for circumcision within the walls of the temple. And just as the teenage Jesus found intellectual and spiritual security within the wisdom and tradition of temple life, so too had John's children found a home away from home within the world of the church. There really was no mystery. Through the waters of baptism, John had given his children to God, steeping them in the spiritual life — and through unfolding patterns of possibility, God took care of the rest.

Our gospel lesson for this morning is framed by two almost identical phrases. Jesus grew in wisdom and in favor — with both God and humanity. Sandwiched in between is this wonderful story about Jesus in the temple — a story about being rooted in a life of faith — rooted in God, rooted in tradition, rooted in spiritual discipline, rooted in something bigger than what we can see and touch and smell and hear. My friends, in the year that stretches ahead of us, let us too root ourselves in a life of faith, being curious and open to the new things God is doing in our lives. The promise is that like Jesus we will grow in wisdom and in favor with both God and humanity.

May it be so, for you and for me. Amen.

New Year's Day
Matthew 25:31-46

When the Son of Man comes in his glory, and all the angels with him, then he will sit on the throne of his glory. All the nations will be gathered before him, and he will separate people one from another as a shepherd separates the sheep from the goats, and he will put the sheep at his right hand and the goats at the left. Then the king will say to those at his right hand, "Come, you that are blessed by my Father, inherit the kingdom prepared for you from the foundation of the world; for I was hungry and you gave me food, I was thirsty and you gave me something to drink, I was a stranger and you welcomed me, I was naked and you gave me clothing, I was sick and you took care of me, I was in prison and you visited me." Then the righteous will answer him, "Lord, when was it that we saw you hungry and gave you food, or thirsty and gave you something to drink? And when was it that we saw you a stranger and welcomed you, or naked and gave you clothing? And when was it that we saw you sick or in prison and visited you?" And the king will answer them, "Truly I tell you, just as you did it to one of the least of these who are members of my family, you did it to me." Then he will say to those at his left hand, "You that are accursed, depart from me into the eternal fire prepared for the devil and his angels; for I was hungry and you gave me no food, I was thirsty and you gave me nothing to drink, I was a stranger and you did not welcome me, naked and you did not give me clothing, sick and in prison and you did not visit me." Then they also will answer, "Lord, when was it that we saw you hungry or thirsty or a stranger or naked or sick or in prison, and did not take care of you?" Then he will answer them, "Truly I tell you, just as you did not do it to one of the least of these, you did not do it to me." And these will go away into eternal punishment, but the righteous into eternal life.

NEW YEAR'S DAY
MATTHEW 25:31-46

SHEEPISH SHALOM

Over 500 hundred years ago, a young man named Francis was living the good life. He was rich, handsome, pampered, popular. And though nominally a Christian, Jesus was a stranger to him. One day, Francis was forced to interact with a loathsome leper. In a moment of dreaded touch, the leper was transformed, literally becoming before his eyes the very image of Christ. And Francis was changed. From that day forward, he felt called to discover the Christ in each person and creature around him, no matter how poor or insignificant they might seem to be. For Saint Francis of Assisi, that day was New Year's Day — the first day of the rest of his life — a dying and a rising to all things new.

It is this kind of transforming imagination that our gospel lesson for this morning has the power to unleash in us. Our text from Matthew is Jesus' final teaching — his final lesson to his disciples and to us before he faced torture and death. There is an urgency in these words. There was a special authority in this vision. This, my friends, is the only version of the last judgment that appears in the gospels and the only one that comes from Jesus' lips.

Old time religion — and increasingly right-wing religion — is religion based not on faith, but on fear. Some of the greatest art in the world depicts the last judgment day in gory, fearful detail — no more spectacularly than Michelangelo's breathtaking mural in the Vatican's Sistine Chapel. With flames, distorted bodies, and anguished faces the artist shows those who are "damned" twisting in the agonies of hell. All the while, in smug, serene safety the "saved" float effortlessly in cloudy heaven. Sitting stoically in the center of this frenetic scene is an impassive Christ, holding a tiny varmint in his fingers, precipitously dangling over the flames of hell. Where will this hapless soul end up? In heaven? Or in hell? Careful study shows that the face of this fragile creature, hanging tenuously from Christ's hand, is the face of Michelangelo. And so, this image is central for the artist, and for all of us who observe the painting. Which way will you go? Which way will I go? Are we sheep, to be embraced by the peace of heaven — or are we goats, destined to writhe in the horrors of hell?

It is interesting to me that Jesus' vision of the last judgment day, as recorded in Matthew, could never be considered the blueprint for Michelangelo's painting. Why? Because Matthew's vision is not a vision based on fear. It is vision based on compassion. And Jesus' image has less to do with the salvation — the judgment — of individuals as it does with the judgment, the salvation of nations. Instead of one terrified soul hanging over the pit of hell, what we see in Matthew 25 are all the nations lined up in front of the throne of heaven. And Jesus is not the one making the pivotal decision. The decision has already been made by those who stand in front of the throne. Both the sheep and the goats — through the actions and decisions of their lives — have *already determined* which direction they will go. Jesus is there simply to render the sentence, not to render the verdict.

Now, before we go any further, let us remind ourselves what the word "salvation" really means. To be "saved" does not mean acceptance into a special club that makes us better and happier than others. No, "salvation" means completion. It means the complete wholeness of abundant life, the blessing of health and justice and joy for everyone. Salvation, in scripture, means the completion of the reign of God. It is a process — the realization of the vision of shalom — rooted in both testaments of the Bible. Jesus' vision of the last judgment was an attempt to provide an answer to a different kind of question: not who will be saved and who will not, but when all is said and done — when the end time finally comes — when you and I are about to breathe our last — what will have really mattered to us — and what will have been the ultimate worth, the ultimate meaning of our lives? Will our lives be judged by how much money we've earned or how many hours we've worked or how many books we've written? Will our lives be judged by how often we've attended church or how many years we've tithed? Will we be "saved" by accepting Jesus Christ as our Lord and Savior? Jesus' answer to all of these questions is a resounding "No!" When all is said and done, the abundance, the wholeness, the meaning of our lives will be judged in one simple way. How well did we respond to human need? How specifically did we feed the hungry, visit the sick, welcome the stranger, clothe the naked, connect with the prisoner? How tangibly did we honor the image of God in our neighbor? The question will not be how well we accepted Jesus into our hearts. The question will be: How well did we embody Jesus in our lives? And if the answer to that question is "Not very well," then we will die unsatisfied, unfulfilled, restless — not because Jesus has judged us, but because we — through our decisions and our lifestyles — have judged ourselves.

There is one detail in this very familiar biblical passage that I noticed for the first time this last week. The sheep — the good guys — in this story — were surprised, they were bewildered, even a bit astonished when Jesus thanked them for feeding him, for visiting him, and for welcoming him. *When did they ever relate to him?* After all, what they did they did instinctively, automatically, freely, not because they were trying to win brownie points, but because it felt good. And they were loving their neighbor, not Jesus. But my friends, this *is* the good news, the surprising news of this story. When we love and serve our neighbor, we automatically love and serve Jesus. When we honor the image of God in each person, then we honor God. It is as simple and wonderful as that.

The Washington Post occasionally has some good heart stuff in its pages. A few years ago I read about a man named Alfred Rascon, the Vietnam veteran who after 33 years of bureaucratic bungling finally received the Congressional Medal of Honor. Rascon was a Mexican immigrant who, because there was no money for college, joined the army when he was seventeen. Trained as a medic, he was assigned to the 173rd Airborne Brigade, which turned out to be the first army combat unit to be sent into South Vietnam. In March of 1966, Rascon's platoon woke up to close and heavy enemy fire. Three times during that ambush, the young Alfred threw his body on top of other soldiers in order to shield them from the fire that pummeled his body instead. At one point a bullet entered his hip, traveled up his spine, and exited by his shoulder. His face was hit and blood poured from his nose and his eyes. But he continued to do his work, protecting soldiers, binding up wounds, even running into direct fire to remove a machine gun from enemy reach. Rascon saved lives that day at a tremendous cost to himself, and his buddies kept on trying to get him the proper recognition he deserved.

The quiet center of this storm today serves as an inspector general for the Selective Service system in northern Virginia. When questioned about his courage and commitment over forty years ago, Rascon seemed surprised by all the fuss: "It has nothing to do with me. It's just a matter of me doing what I had to do that day like any other day. I am dumbfounded by these guys who remember that day and haven't given up. It's an honor to realize how much they still care for me." Like the sheep in today's vision who end up in the kingdom of God, Alfred Rascon was astonished by the positive reward that now, years later, he received. Like any ordinary person he was just doing what people are supposed to do — rejoicing in the gift of his own life, and honoring the gift of life in others.

My friends, how we choose to use our time, our energy, our wealth, and our talents has everything to do with how abundant our lives will eventually turn out to be — not abundant in "stuff" but abundant in love and grace. Every time we visit our aged mother, volunteer in our child's classroom, bring in generous amounts of non-perishable food for thanksgiving baskets, volunteer at a soup kitchen, take a moment to greet that visitor sitting in the pew next to us, write an extravagant check for disaster relief in Haiti, we are promoting shalom. We are promoting the vision of harmony and wholeness that God offers us in scripture. And we do it not because we have to but because we want to and because as God's ambassadors, we need to.

But, my friends, let us be reminded again that according to Matthew's vision, individual, one-on-one effort is not enough. Remember that it is not individuals who are sentenced and saved in this vision. It is the nations. And as citizens of this nation, we must care about how our nation as a whole is doing the work of shalom.

Feed the hungry. How are we doing in child nutrition programs, international debt relief, foreign aid to countries that really need it — not just countries that serve our national interest? *Visit the sick.* Why is it that guaranteed national health coverage continues to be a nasty partisan fight? *Welcome the stranger.* How hard are we working as a congregation to encourage humane and hospitable immigration reform in this country? Brothers and sisters, when we refuse to consider these corporate justice issues — these social, "nation-based" problems — we are, according to today's text, refusing to serve Jesus. And as a result, we are excluding ourselves and others from the abundant life that Jesus has come to offer.

The final good news in today's story is that this vivid picture which Jesus paints for us is a vision. It is a future possibility not yet a present reality. We still have time to reexamine our lives. We still have time to recreate our values and priorities, not because we want to be "saved," but because we yearn for the meaning, the purpose, the wholeness which only compassionate service in Christ's name can bring.

And Jesus said, "If you have done it unto one of the least of these, you have done it unto me." It's not rocket science, my friends. It's just simple caring. This is our call and this is our purpose. And this is the one sure path to full and abundant life.

May it be so for you and for me. Amen.

Christmas 2
John 1:(1-9) 10-18

He was in the world, and the world came into being through him; yet the world did not know him. He came to what was his own, and his own people did not accept him. But to all who received him, who believed in his name, he gave power to become children of God, who were born, not of blood or of the will of the flesh or of the will of man, but of God. And the Word became flesh and lived among us, and we have seen his glory, the glory as of a father's only son, full of grace and truth. (John testified to him and cried out, "This was he of whom I said, 'He who comes after me ranks ahead of me because he was before me.' ") From his fullness we have all received, grace upon grace. The law indeed was given through Moses; grace and truth came through Jesus Christ. No one has ever seen God. It is God the only Son, who is close to the Father's heart, who has made him known.

CHRISTMAS 2
JOHN 1:(1-9) 10-18

LIGHT LIVING

The best way to respond to today's scripture reading is to say nothing — to let it stand in all its elegance, its mystery, its power. But being a preacher, I am genetically unable to say nothing. So I will try to share with you my deep need and my deep affection for this particular passage of God's holy word. This is what John says to me, and so to you, this first Sunday in the new year.

In the beginning — back before our imaginations can imagine
in the beginning — there was darkness —
deep dazzling darkness.
And in the center of this deep dark womb was God
a warm wonderful Word, the pulsing Word of Life.

And then out of the dazzling darkness
came dazzling light —
stars, bursting sun, glowing moon
a holy metamorphosis.
Dazzling light out of dazzling darkness.
This was the light of the first creation.

But then there was the light of the second creation.
Out of God's warm wonderful wordy womb came flesh,
a holy wholeness with skin on
glowing with light, glaring and glorious

a human God — full of grace and truth. The grace to heal us.
And the truth to refine us.

And so with no effort on our part,
we were — we are — given a second chance. And the other kind of darkness —
the dull, desperate, dangerous kind of darkness —
so different from God's dazzling darkness
the dull, desperate, dangerous kind of darkness has never been able to overcome the dazzling light of incarnation.

I have become afflicted in middle age with a craving for the darkness. No matter when I go to bed, no matter how tired I am, no matter if I am on vacation or enjoying a day off, no matter, I wake up each day in the darkness. I crawl out of bed in the darkness. I creep around the house in the darkness. I light a candle in the darkness. And I find more security than at any other point in the day. It is in that early morning darkness that I most intimately encounter God — a breath beyond the silence, a glimmer beyond the shadow, a presence hovering just beyond reach. It is a presence that promises to push me, to play with me, to protect me in the possibilities that stretch before me. And when the light slowly comes, creeping into my day, creeping into my heart, it reveals what has been there all along. What I have discovered is that light does not bring anything new; light just reveals what has always been there.

The Jewish people have long known how to honor the darkness. The Jewish sabbath begins at sundown — twelve hours of darkness are sanctified even before the first smudge of dawn. They know that darkness is the womb of light. In many ways that honors the pattern of our biblical story. Even agnostic scientists will agree that life and light were born out of cosmic darkness. And it was the darkness of Mount Sinai that gave birth to the Ten Commandments. It was the darkness of the cave that gave birth to Elijah's hope. It was the darkness of Mary's womb that gave birth to the Messiah. It was the darkness of Gethsemane that gave birth to Jesus' courage. It was the darkness of the cross that gave birth to God's unconditional love. And it was the darkness of the tomb that provided the womb of resurrection.

Modern television served us well on the birth of the new millennium on January 1, 2000, as images of human hope, and a bit of human hubris, were beamed to us from around the world. Twenty hours of millennium marvels played with our human senses, as dance and music and vision rippled slowly across the globe. Every one of those celebrations from Mali to San Francisco, from South Africa to the tiptop village in Norway, from Manger Square in Bethlehem to the National Mall in Washington — every one of these celebrations started in the darkness — in the dazzling darkness — that is God's home just as surely is the light. Then in a thousand creative ways, explosions of pyrotechnics shattered the darkness dramatically. Explosions of hope. Explosions of excess. Explosions of joy and peace and love. Human explosions, which, of course, lasted for only a few minutes. And then God's dazzling darkness reclaimed the moment — a darkness waiting for *God* to bring the lasting light — in God's own time, and God's own way.

My friends, the apostle Paul, again and again, reminds us that we have a choice. We can be children of darkness. Or we can be children of light. Trust in Jesus Christ makes all the difference. But the simple point I want to make today is that we cannot be children of light if we don't begin in the darkness. If we don't befriend the darkness, if we don't trust the darkness, for God lives in the darkness just as certainly as God lives in the light. The dazzling darkness of mystery. But also the full, dangerous darkness of human despair and decay.

When the first millennium rolled into the second millennium during the Middle Ages, the world was indeed a dark place. First and foremost, there was the fanatical darkness of the Christian church that oppressed the poor, kept the peasants illiterate, and buried the light of knowledge far away in the bowels of the monasteries. This same fanatical darkness led to the bloody, bitter Crusades — an eruption of evil out of which religious intolerance has been gushing ever since.

Many recent commentaries have suggested that now as we move into the third millennium, things are different. The darkness of our human infancy has been vanquished, and we are glowing in the light of an invigorating dawn. Certainly the rising markets and the growing global partnerships indicate that life is pretty good for some of us. But let us not deceive ourselves. The dull dangerous darkness of human despair and decay *is* still around us. All the carnage and hate in Gaza and Israel, in Syria and the Sudan, in Iraq and Afghanistan, show how dark is the darkness still hiding in the human soul.

When Nelson Mandela was still alive, he was one of the few voices looking honestly at the state of the world in which we live. While some optimists suggest that the modern era is a time to celebrate, Mandela quietly reminded us with the dignity and integrity that marked his entire life that: "We live in a time where most people are still languishing in poverty, most people are still subjected to hunger, preventable disease, illiteracy, and insufficient shelter." Much has been made about the stellar number of millionaires who now live in this country — over 3.5 million. But we need to acknowledge that despite all this newfound wealth, 16% of our people still live in poverty — a greater percentage of impoverished citizens than those who lived in America in 1900. Is *that* progress?

Today the gospel writer tries to give expression to the texture of light and darkness that make up our human life and to the hope which Jesus the Christ weaves into that eternal pattern. In a moment of inspiration and passionate love, God spoke a fleshy word, shouting out of the darkness — piercing, permeating, pulverizing the darkness with light — a light every bit as dramatic and explosive as July Fourth and of New Year's Eve combined. John never claims that the darkness disappears. Rather he simply promises that the light of incarnation — the light of God down here in the midst of us — this light will always be stronger than the darkness. This light will always give definition to the shadows of our lives. This light will always keep us company in the deep darkness of the night.

The preacher Bill Carter tells the story about a friend named Tom, who as a teenager found himself, one foolish night, running from the police. He had done nothing wrong, but he was caught in an alley in a bad section of town. A searchlight was turned on, and Tom panicked. Running down an alley, he jumped behind a trash can. But the police kept coming, and they demanded that Tom come from behind the trash can. Tom stood up, trembling, covered with garbage. When asked what he was doing, Tom said that he was frightened by the searchlight — afraid that the police would think he had done something wrong. So he panicked and hid. As the police confronted him, Tom was sure he would be arrested for disturbing the peace and his parents would be told. But then the police officer set his heart at ease: ""Son, I am not here to arrest you. I am here to protect you." Carter wrote:

> *As he stood before that searchlight, Tom says he caught a glimpse of what it means to stand before Jesus, who is the light of the world. There he was fully exposed yet completely protected. He was fully revealed yet free from unnecessary punishment. He stood hip-deep in garbage, yet cleaner than he had ever felt... In that moment he saw*

something of what it means to stand in the presence of Jesus Christ, who is full of truth, but also full of grace.[1]

My friends, Jesus, the fleshy word, shouts and shines in the darkness, and though the darkness is very real and human, and absolutely essential in order to reveal the light, even so, the darkness will never overcome the light of the world.

This is the good news of the gospel, freshly spoken for a new year in a very frightening world.

May it be so for you and for me. Amen.

---

1. Bill Carter, *Lectionary Homiletics*, January 2000.

Epiphany of Our Lord
Matthew 2:1-12

In the time of King Herod, after Jesus was born in Bethlehem of Judea, wise men from the East came to Jerusalem, asking, "Where is the child who has been born king of the Jews? For we observed his star at its rising, and have come to pay him homage." When King Herod heard this, he was frightened, and all Jerusalem with him; and calling together all the chief priests and scribes of the people, he inquired of them where the Messiah was to be born. They told him, "In Bethlehem of Judea; for so it has been written by the prophet: 'And you, Bethlehem, in the land of Judah, are by no means least among the rulers of Judah; for from you shall come a ruler who is to shepherd my people Israel.'" Then Herod secretly called for the wise men and learned from them the exact time when the star had appeared. Then he sent them to Bethlehem, saying, "Go and search diligently for the child; and when you have found him, bring me word so that I may also go and pay him homage." When they had heard the king, they set out; and there, ahead of them, went the star that they had seen at its rising, until it stopped over the place where the child was. When they saw that the star had stopped, they were overwhelmed with joy. On entering the house, they saw the child with Mary his mother; and they knelt down and paid him homage. Then, opening their treasure chests, they offered him gifts of gold, frankincense, and myrrh. And having been warned in a dream not to return to Herod, they left for their own country by another road.

Epiphany of Our Lord
Matthew 2:1-12

How Intelligent Is God's Design?

I wonder. I wonder how the wise men would react to our current controversy over intelligent design. I wonder how these sages, who were the educated intellectuals and sophisticated scientists of their day would react to this public tug of war? On the one side are those who see creation as a random process of nature. On the other side are those who see creation as the intentional plan of a designer God. I wonder if the wise men would find it difficult to reconcile the facts of science with the imagination of faith? Or would they find a way to embrace both as part of the mystery of life?

It seems that even Charles Darwin was caught in the ambiguities of faith and science. In 1880, when he published his world-changing book *On the Origen of Species*, the critics swiftly accused him of apostasy and atheism. Darwin's good friend was Asa Gray, a distinguished Harvard botanist, who was also a faithful believing Christian. Gray quickly jumped to his friend's defense, favorably reviewing Darwin's controversial study. But, in private, the two friends carried on a lively debate. Gray tried to persuade Darwin to accept a "harmony of evolution with a belief in intelligent design." The Harvard professor was convinced that "variation does not always seem an accident, but often is 'guided in certain lines,' as if by an intelligent power." Because Gray was familiar with scripture, he understood and trusted the attributes of a benevolent God. He was able to accept the suffering and the evil found in nature as compatible with a loving God.

Darwin, on the other hand, interpreted these darker sides of creation as errors, which led to his notion of the randomness of evolution. For Darwin, the chaotic patterns of natural selection led to the survival of some species and the demise of others. And yet the agnostic Darwin was also able to write the following in a letter to his friend:

> *I can see no reason why a man, or other animal, may not have been aboriginally produced by other laws, and that all these laws may have been expressly designed by an omniscient Creator... But the more I think, the more bewildered I become.*[1]

Bewildered; that is how I feel much of the time when confronted with the complexity of creation and the complexity of a loving God who *does* somehow allow pain and suffering to exist. Bewilderment but also wonderment. Wonderment, whenever I find myself teetering on the edge of elegance, teetering on the edge of mystery — whenever I reach a point where my mind can no longer understand where my heart is leading me.

I am not much of a scientist, which may be obvious to many of you. After all, the only reason I passed physics in high school was because I finished all my experiments, and put a fancy cover on my lab reports! But I remember clearly the day I experienced an epiphany in my limited realm of scientific wonder. It was during my sabbatical a few years ago, and I was spending some time in Rocky Mountain National Park. I had driven to the highest point on that breathtaking highway that winds through those magnificent peaks. I stopped to take a walk on the path rising above the visitor's center. Suddenly my eyes were drawn toward some small plants blooming on the side of the path — rather homely plants, with squat thick leaves, tiny flowers, hovering, clinging almost desperately to the rocky soil. Why such an odd shape? I wondered. And then I remembered the educational display I had seen in the visitor's center, explaining that the thirsty leaves and the deep roots and the low embrace of these plants insure that the flowers will bloom — that they will survive the cold brutality of the winter and the dry winds of the summer. Immediately, I felt a jolt of awe. Wow! An utterly unique design for this particular place and this particular plant. It was only after I experienced the wonder in my heart that I was able to move into the wonder of my mind, and the questions began to bubble up. Why? How? Who?

The wise men in Matthew's story — *magios* in the Greek — according to biblical scholars, are astrologers and dream interpreters — which makes them suspect in the contemporary world of science. After all, you and I may secretly check our horoscope every day, but we are smart enough not to give rational credence to what the positioning of the stars predict. But in first-century Persia, studying the patterns and the design of the heavens was advanced science, particularly when a new star or comet or light interrupted the predictable patterns of the past. Our wise men are also steeped in the sacred writings of the both the East and the West — perhaps some of the first scholars of world religion. These sacred writings suggest that a new light or star is a portent — a sign pointing to the birth of something, or someone, important. Specifically, though they are non-Jews, the Magi are familiar with the Hebrew texts, similar to the one from Isaiah this morning, that predicts a star as a portent of the Messiah, of the anointed one. The text predicts a sign pointing toward the mighty one who will come to save the Jewish people and complete God's complex work of creation.

When this spectacular new star actually appears in the western sky, the Magi take off. With curiosity and courage they follow the star, utilizing all the intellectual, scientific knowledge they can muster. But the purpose of their journey is clearly articulated by Matthew. They travel in order to pay homage. They journey — according to Webster's definition of "homage" — to offer "reverence and respect and honor" to whatever or whomever their knowledge had led them. It is there, of course, at the frontier of their intellectual knowing, that the wise men discover mystery. It is there that they discover the mighty one — the God of power — enfleshed in the powerless innocence of a baby. Stunned — surprised — unable to understand with their minds, the Magi instead seek understanding with their hearts. Bewilderment turns into wonderment. They kneel. They bow down. They worship. They offer love, because logic no longer makes sense.

Tim Shriver, who has served as the president of the Special Olympics, is part of the Kennedy clan, and the son of Sargent Shriver who served as director of the Peace Corps during the Kennedy administration. The senior Shriver was also a victim of Alzheimer's disease. Because of his cousin Kathleen Kennedy's mental disability, and because of his father's mental diminishment, Tim Shriver has become particularly attuned to the inevitable vulnerabilities of the human condition. And so through the Special Olympics he has focused on the human dignity of people with disabilities. In an essay about Christmas, Tim has this to say:

> When intelligent design... seem[s] to be the focus of public religious activism, Christmas is like a celebration from another world. It is difficult, after all, to see a case for intelligent design in Bethlehem. Who would believe that the wise and powerful God of intelligent design would adopt the vulnerability of a shivering infant as his incarnational calling card? ... Christmas is more mystery than design, more unintelligent than intelligent, more question than answer... And deep spiritual questions should be the foundation of faith in the public square... Mystery suggests a

> *call to public action in search of God's ways... science, with all its majesty and achievement, has only one thing in common with religion: When it reaches its most profound questions, it, too, yields to mystery.*[2]

I have come to believe in my own journey of faith that God lives in the questions. I believe that seeking understanding with my mind is the preparation I need to trust with my heart. I believe that faith is the frontier beyond the limits of knowledge. I have started looking for portents — in the sky, in the newspaper, in the textbooks, in the science lab, in the hospital room, in the darkness as well as the light. Yes, I have started looking for those signs of a God who is trying to do a new thing. I have discovered that it is in the process, in the journey, and in the questions that new knowledge and new understanding is usually found. Specifically in this peculiar American controversy about intelligent design, I have come to believe that evolution *is* intelligent design. And the intelligent designer *is* the *one* whom I call God. Yes, it is in the chaos of creation and the unfolding randomness of adaptation and change that God is bringing this world into the fullness of its design.

This faith claim that I feel in my bones is exactly that — a faith claim. Evolution is science. The wonder that leads to trust in a benevolent intelligent designer is faith. Science belongs in the classroom. Faith does not because no curriculum can — or should — define the mystery of the soul.

It is in my personal spiritual journey that I seek to weave together the wonders of faith and science. And I believe that this pattern of natural growth we see in physical evolution is also the template for spiritual growth — for spiritual evolution. It is in the random events of my life and yours that God is at work unfolding our potential and our promise through events and processes that we can neither create nor control. Given this chaotic, unpredictable evolution of the spirit, each of us has a choice. Like Herod we can resist the providence and grace of God, clinging to our pretense of power and control. Or like the wise men, we can follow the star of surprise, trusting in the journey and paying homage to the mysteries we find along the way.

In the world of Celtic spirituality, there is a folk expression, "Heaven is only a foot and a half above the height of our heads." But according to Quaker writer Edward Hays, the real location of heaven is a foot and a half *below* the height of our heads. It is found in our hearts. The secular is steeped in the sacred. If we are not prepared to see God hidden in the world, then we often miss the presence of the holy. And so, it is only when we search, when we journey into the mysterious frontiers of our mind, when we explore the secret places of our heart, it is only then that we find the God who has chosen to become with us, and for us, and one of us.

Let me finish with a story about a rabbi and his son:

> *One day a young boy came into the house after a game of hide-and-seek, with tears streaming down his face. His father took the child into his arms and asked what was wrong. The child tearfully explained that he and the other children had been playing hide-and-seek and that he had hidden himself, but no one had come seeking him. The father kissed his small son lovingly and said, "My child, now you know how God feels. For God is hidden in our midst and waits patiently for us to begin the search."*[3]

Friends, this Epiphany Sunday let us arise and shine. Let us arise and join the Magi, seeking the new thing God is always doing in our midst. And in the random wonder of the

journey may we worship the mysterious and the mundane as intelligently and reverently as possible.
May it be so for you and for me. Amen.

———————

1. James Dao, "Intelligent Design: The Descent of a Concept," *Wall Street Journal*, date unknown.

2. "In the Presence of Mystery," *The Washington Post*, 12/05.

3. Source unknown.

Baptism of Our Lord
Luke 3:15-17, 21-22

As the people were filled with expectation, and all were questioning in their hearts concerning John, whether he might be the Messiah, John answered all of them by saying, "I baptize you with water; but one who is more powerful than I is coming; I am not worthy to untie the thong of his sandals. He will baptize you with the Holy Spirit and fire. His winnowing fork is in his hand, to clear his threshing floor and to gather the wheat into his granary; but the chaff he will burn with unquenchable fire." ... Now when all the people were baptized, and when Jesus also had been baptized and was praying, the heaven was opened, and the Holy Spirit descended upon him in bodily form like a dove. And a voice came from heaven, "You are my Son, the Beloved; with you I am well pleased."

BAPTISM OF OUR LORD
LUKE 3:15-17, 21-22

THE THREE BS

Barbara Brown Taylor tells a story about her grandmother Lucy. Lucy was a very strange looking woman. She had lost both her legs to diabetes and had wooden stumps where limbs should be. Her weak eyes demanded that she wear dark glasses and most of the time she looked like a disabled bomber pilot. But to her granddaughters, Lucy was wonderful. Whenever Barbara would visit her grandmother, grace would abound. In the closet would be wrapped packages — enough for a surprise each day of the visit. The meals were delicious — always with a favorite dessert. And then there were the shopping trips — to buy dresses and crinolines and new hair bows. But the best part of these visits were the baths. Each night Grandma Lucy would draw a hot bath filled with suds and with her big sponge she would polish Barbara's skin. Then, following the bath she would anoint her granddaughter's body with Jergens® lotion — all the way down to the soles of her feet. The perfect ending would be the Evening in Paris dusting powder — when Lucy would tickle Barbara's body with a pale blue powder puff. Barbara writes:

> *When grandma Lucy was done, I knew that I was precious. I was absolutely convinced that I was loved and nothing has happened since to shake that conviction.*[1]

My own story is not nearly as exotic, but to me it felt the same. As a small child my asthma attacks would usually hit in the middle of the night and my gasping for breath would quickly escalate into panic. Quick trips to the emergency room followed and then the long hours in the oxygen tent until my lungs could be stabilized. But always with me was my father — carrying me, holding me, staying with me, and I felt loved. In my smallness, in my sickness, in my weakness, in my imperfectness, I felt loved not because I was safe but because I was loved — "precious" as Barbara Brown puts it — and nothing has happened since to shake my conviction. For both of us it was these early experiences of trust that helped us figure out the meaning of faith, which is after all nothing more and nothing less than trust. It is trusting God no matter what.

This morning our scripture passages give us two different pictures of God. One is a picture of might. The other is a picture of mercy. One presents a God of glory, the other presents a God of grace. One in bold palette presents a vivid Lord of lightning and the other, in softer tones, gives us a lavish Lord of love. And both of these pictures are true. In Psalm 29 we meet the voice — the powerful voice, the majestic voice, the voice that thunders, that breaks the cedars, that flashes forth making oaks to whirl, stripping the forest bare. This God is not a God to mess with, not a God to mutter about, not a God to meddle with.

In our gospel lesson, when we meet John the Baptist, we see that he clearly worshiped this kind of mammoth, mighty, master God. And he worried that the Messiah-to-come would sweep into the wilderness like a refiner's fire consuming human sin as if it were twigs in a tinder box.

But much to John's surprise — and perhaps disappointment — the God he expected was not the God who arrived. The mighty Messiah turned out to be the gentle Jesus. Rather than a military man lording it over his subjects, we meet instead, a modest man, who waded into muddy water, choosing to be a companion with those he had come to serve. The two conflicting images of the Holy Spirit included in Luke's passage underline the difference between John's expectation and the reality of Jesus. For John the Baptist, the Holy Spirit was like a ferocious fire, representing the judgment of God. But when the Holy Spirit came upon Jesus, it was like a dove — like the Noah's Ark dove that marked the end of God's judgment. The fire God, the ire God is replaced by the dove God, the love God.

In all of the gospel accounts describing the baptism of Jesus, one question remains unanswered. Why was Jesus baptized? Why did he need to be baptized? After all, according to John, baptism was for the purpose of repentance and the forgiveness of sins. Of what did Jesus need to repent? And what did he need to be forgiven for? Actually, when you think about it, this one who was to be baptized by fire never baptized anyone else. Instead, Jesus submitted to the waters of baptism kneeling in the mud and the muck and the mire. Why? For the same reason he was born in a manger, that he ate with prostitutes and tax collectors, that he cried and prayed and slept in a garden, that he died a painful, very human death. Quite simply Jesus came to be like us, so we could grow to be like him. Jesus was baptized into our humanity, so that we can be baptized into his divinity.

In the Eastern Orthodox tradition, those who are baptized in the same font become siblings — they are considered the same flesh and blood — they are kin with one another. In this sense, Jesus became siblings with the crowd and with all those with whom he was baptized in the River Jordan. When we are baptized into Christ in the waters of this font, we too become siblings with Christ and with one another. The personal name we receive is important. But much more important is the spiritual name we receive — Christian: bearer of Christ — brother and sister of Christ.

There is the story that a Presbyterian pastor tells about one of those embarrassing moments in ministry. He was in the middle of performing a wedding ceremony, just about to lead the couple through their vows when suddenly he forgot the name of the groom. Trying to cover the awkward moment, the pastor asked the groom with great solemnity "With what name were you baptized?" The groom, a bit taken aback, paused. But with great confidence, he responded, "I was baptized with the name of our Lord Jesus Christ!" This didn't help the pastor much — but at least this guy understood the meaning of baptism![2]

What is most important about our text for today is how it ends. After this remarkable transformation from thunder theology into tender theology — after the metamorphosis of this abstract, awesome God into a fragile, flesh and blood God — after the heavenly one decided to become earthy — to become concrete in bushes that burn and babies that burp and birds that baptize — it is then that the Creator God responded in a very particular way. Quite simply, God was delighted!

If you have ever wondered if God is a mean God or a merciful God — if you have ever worried that God may blast us instead of bless us — if you ever have thought that God is a God of law more than God of love, Luke 3:22 alleviates that confusion. The voice of God speaks once again. But unlike the megaphone voice of Psalm 29 this voice is warm and welcoming. "You are my Son, the Beloved One; with you I am well pleased." To the man in the mud, this Son who has become a servant, God speaks. Even before Jesus has done anything noteworthy or worthwhile God praises him. God affirms that Jesus is precious, that he is unique, that he is loved — not for what he does but for who he is.

In this baptism scene, God echoed the divine delight and pleasure that was expressed in the very beginning days of creation. After the creation of the sea and the dry land, God said, "It is good." After the creation of the light and the dark, the stars, sun, and moon, God said, "It is good." After the creation of the birds and the animals, the plants, the trees, and the fish of the sea, God said, "It is very good." And after the creation of man and woman in God's image, God said, "It is good. It is very, very good." After the baptism of Jesus, after this total immersion into the human condition, God says, "This is good. This is delightful. This is the beloved, who brings me great pleasure. This is very, very good." And so it is with each one of us when we are baptized. We too are blessed as the beloved. We too bring pleasure to God.

The Greek word for baptism means: "To dip, to immerse, to submerge, and (my favorite) to saturate." Baptism is, for all of us the bath of the beloved, when God takes pleasure in saturating us. God is saturating us with water, saturating us with grace, saturating us with blessing. When I read about Jesus' baptism, what I understand is happening is very different than what traditional doctrines have explained. Rather than saving us from original sin, Jesus' baptism mirrors for us our original blessing — encouraging us to become servants of love — offering blessing, and not judgment, to others. Despite the fact that we remain partial, sinful, fragile, imperfect people, our original blessing can empower us if we remember that we are baptized.

This morning we celebrate the ordination into full-time ministry for all of us and that is really what baptism is all about. Through this saturation of blessing and of belonging, we become the beloved — those set apart by God's love to become love in the world. Every time we baptize an infant or an adult, each of us is reminded of our original blessing — reminded of the waters of baptism that have washed over our lives and each of us is reminded of God's voice in our lives.

"You are my child, the Beloved with whom I am well pleased."

Remember your baptism, my friends. Remember that you are blessed. Remember that you belong. Remember that you are the beloved. And remember that it is a gracious God who has taken delight and pleasure in who you are and who you are becoming. This profound gift changes us. This profound gift defines us. This profound gift is what we have to share with the world. How can we do anything else but be a blessing to others? This is the gift of this day. This is the good news of this day. This is the call of this day. And it is very, very good.

May it be so for you and for me. Amen.

---

1. *The Preaching Life* (Cambridge, Massachusetts: Cowley Publications, 1993), p. 17.

2. Marj Carpenter, *The Presbyterian Outlook*, January 5-11, 1998, p. 2.

Epiphany 2
John 2:1-11

On the third day there was a wedding in Cana of Galilee, and the mother of Jesus was there. Jesus and his disciples had also been invited to the wedding. When the wine gave out, the mother of Jesus said to him, "They have no wine." And Jesus said to her, "Woman, what concern is that to you and to me? My hour has not yet come." His mother said to the servants, "Do whatever he tells you." Now standing there were six stone water jars for the Jewish rites of purification, each holding twenty or thirty gallons. Jesus said to them, "Fill the jars with water." And they filled them up to the brim. He said to them, "Now draw some out, and take it to the chief steward." So they took it. When the steward tasted the water that had become wine, and did not know where it came from (though the servants who had drawn the water knew), the steward called the bridegroom and said to him, "Everyone serves the good wine first, and then the inferior wine after the guests have become drunk. But you have kept the good wine until now." Jesus did this, the first of his signs, in Cana of Galilee, and revealed his glory; and his disciples believed in him.

Epiphany 2
John 2:1-11

Is God Invited?

We could always count on it. Every year, on the second Sunday of January, my dad would preach his drinking sermon — or, I should say his anti-drinking sermon. Having seen firsthand in my mother's family the deathly cost of drunkenness, having spent more nights than he could remember offering pastoral support to families dealing with the fall-out of alcohol, Dad was convinced that alcohol was a demon. It was all too often the destroyer of the abundant life which God gives us to cherish. His message was pretty simple. If our bodies are the temple of the Holy Spirit, as Paul so poignantly reminds us, then when we pollute our bodies with excessive alcohol, we are defaming the very dwelling place of God. He was right and still is.

Saturating the majority of automobile accidents, soaking the fabric of much domestic violence, floating maliciously in the center of many cases of heart disease and cancer are the toxic remnants of alcohol. In a past issue of the *Duke Alumni Magazine*, then President Nan Keohane offers a breathtakingly honest look at current alcohol use on college campuses. Every year, over 30,000 students are treated for acute alcohol poisoning. In one survey, it was discovered that on the Duke campus, 41% of all students reported binge drinking within the previous two weeks. Of the students, 28% reported having blacked out and 20% of the students had driven while drunk. A common feature at Duke parties was a 100-gallon trash can lined with plastic intended to receive vomit. Now,

Duke is no worse than most college campuses — and better than some. We know that if alcohol was not so central to our culture, to our economy, to our adult behavior, these college statistics would not be so high. And the overall destruction of alcohol would not be so devastating.

All of which makes our morning gospel lesson problematic. Obviously, my father never used *this* text as the basis for his annual temperance sermons. John's story of the wedding at Cana is vivid. In his debut as the power and presence of God, Jesus literally drowns us with wine and no matter how hard we try to "spiritualize" this story, there is no way we can hide 150 gallons of vintage rose. So, what is going on?

Eastern hospitality is a wonder to behold. In Jesus' day the customs of hospitality were clear. Every village home had big jars of water at the entrance way to provide ready relief from the journey. Feet were washed the moment a guest arrived and then water was readily available for hand washing not only before meals but in between each course. With a large wedding crowd expected, the host stacked six water jars by the door — just in case. Weddings in first-century Palestine were amazing events. They usually lasted a week and the groom was responsible for providing food and drink through it all.

Wine, in those days, was the drink of choice and of necessity. The water was simply not pure enough to drink. But let us be clear what this vino was like — two parts wine to three parts water — sweet, tame, and thin by today's frat party standards. As is the case in most Middle Eastern and European countries today, such common use of wine made drunkenness very uncommon and much more socially condemned than it is in our own alcohol confused culture. If we put all of this in context, it probably never occurred to Jesus that by transforming so much water into wine, he was offering a problematic sign and a problematic message. My friends, alcohol abuse is a uniquely third-millennium problem that was simply not part of the picture in first-century Palestine.

Today's gospel text is not fair fodder for arguments about alcohol consumption or about who should drink, at what age, in what amount. At the same time, to use this text to justify unhealthy behavior is simply missing the point. So what is the point?

Today's gospel text is about the very nature of God and about the very purpose of being human. The nature of God is pure grace — generous, abundant, excessive, surprising grace — grace overflowing to the brim — in times and places when we least expect it. And the purpose of being human is to long for this grace, this joy, this abundance — to thirst for God until we are finally satisfied. The French philosopher Blaise Pascal once said that the core of human identity is what he described as a God-shaped vacuum — and we are restless until that void is filled. One writer described this human longing in this way:

> *Our thirst for God will never be satisfied by taking an eye-dropper-ful of divine love and dribbling it onto our tongues... We want to swing out on a rope over the river, and let go, and splash naked into the deep, delightful pool... that is our thirst for God.*[1]

As Christians, we believe that this insatiable thirst for God can be satisfied by Jesus — by his palpable presence, by his compassionate power, by his healing generosity. The gospel stories give us this Jesus and if we open our hearts we can meet him at weddings and at funerals. We can meet him in the temple and in the marketplace. We can meet him on our marriage bed and on our death bed. We can meet him in our homes and in our offices. And most of all, we can meet him in the dark night of our soul.

The wedding at Cana has become one of my favorite gospel stories because it offers me two rich and dependable promises that give flesh to Isaiah's words this morning — the bold proclamation that we are the very delight of God.

The first promise is this. Because Jesus "domesticates God" in the very daily-ness of life, we can expect to find the extraordinary in the ordinary. We can expect to discover the holy in the mundane. We can expect to glimpse God in the humble clay of humanity.

Even when life is simple and mundane, God is filling us to the brim with possibility, grace, and joy — not happiness, but joy. Yes, God is filling us with the very elegance of breath and love and emotion — a wine rich enough to savor even on the bleakest day.

The second promise I receive from Jesus in today's story becomes more precious the older I get. The promise is this: God saves the best for last. Despite my doubt and impatience, God has indeed proven this promise to be true. If you are like me, you have mourned the passing of each stage of your life. The simplicity of childhood is gone, the beauty of adolescence has faded, the freedom of college is over, the ambition of young adulthood has dwindled, the ardor of marriage has cooled, the exhausting delight of parenting has slowed down, the body is creaky, parents are dying and dead. You know the refrain — the best of life has already passed us by and we wallow in nostalgia.

Except that God keeps surprising us with *new* wine that is sweeter and tastier than that which has come before. Yes, I can't move quite as fast or do quite as much — but the slower pace helps me savor each moment more fully. Yes, there is too much pain, disappointment, and failure in the world, but allowing rich emotion to flow honestly through me makes the beautiful and the lovely all that much more precious. Yes, the day-to-day craziness of car pools and lunches, homework and curfews is over — but the newfound distance gives me the delicious freedom to finally admit that I am not in charge of my children's lives. Yes, the wine is sweeter and the aroma more pleasing the older I get. Such is the generosity of God's amazing grace in our lives.

I remember paying a visit to Tom and Opal Ward — 89 and 91 respectively — living with their daughter and her husband. When I arrived Tom was curled up in bed snuggled into his blanket like a little boy content, warm, and cozy. Remembering his feisty, peripatetic, sometimes overwhelming presence just ten years ago, I was somewhat startled. But I was also touched by this new, diminutive Tom. We no longer could converse about philosophy or theology like we used to — about the cosmic nature of Christ and the intricate affair going on between religion and science in the post-modern world. Such exotic thinking was, for Tom, a thing of the past. But we could, and we did, talk about God almighty and about being "elegant." Yes, for those who knew him, such phrases still rolled off Tom's tongue.

At one point, Tom suddenly smiled and his eyes lit up. He talked about the tremendous blessings of his life, despite his many failings. He talked about the specific joy of having been married to Opal for 64 years. Rather than complaining about his old age, rather than bemoaning his useless body, instead of wishing that things were better, Tom simply glowed with the rock bottom knowledge that he had been blessed and continued to be blessed by the simple gifts of life. If that's what hardening of the arteries does, then may it happen to all of us so that we too can savor every last drop of the ever new wine of God's grace.

My friends, life is a party and God is the host. May we invite God into all the places of our living and may we glorify God and enjoy God forever.

May it be so, for you and for me. Amen.

1. David Rensberger, "Thirst for God," *Weavings*, July 2000, p. 23.

Epiphany 3
Luke 4:14-21

Then Jesus, filled with the power of the Spirit, returned to Galilee, and a report about him spread through all the surrounding country. He began to teach in their synagogues and was praised by everyone. When he came to Nazareth, where he had been brought up, he went to the synagogue on the sabbath day, as was his custom. He stood up to read, and the scroll of the prophet Isaiah was given to him. He unrolled the scroll and found the place where it was written: "The Spirit of the Lord is upon me, because he has anointed me to bring good news to the poor. He has sent me to proclaim release to the captives and recovery of sight to the blind, to let the oppressed go free, to proclaim the year of the Lord's favor." And he rolled up the scroll, gave it back to the attendant, and sat down. The eyes of all in the synagogue were fixed on him. Then he began to say to them, "Today this scripture has been fulfilled in your hearing."

Epiphany 3
Luke 4:14-21

A Justice Jesus

When I did my doctoral studies in organizational revitalization, we were taught a simple way to bring about transformation in the way ministry is done. Simply change the name of the committees or create a brand new structure to do new things in new ways. In one of the parishes I served, we re-envisioned our ministry every five years. One year, more to humor me than anything else, the Vision Task Force agreed to propose a new name for our mission outreach committee changing it from Church and Society Committee to the Social Justice Committee. They were sure, however, that this would get shot down when the Session got to voting on the plan. And, by golly, they were right! With unanimous energy and voice, the session removed or obliterated the word justice. Clearly, according to those elders, no politically sensitive jargon belongs in any organizational plan.

What is it about the word "justice" that turns us off? Is it because it sounds legalistic, moralistic, or judgmental? Is it because of recent events surrounding the Justices of the Supreme Court that remind us of how political the word "justice" can become? Or is it merely the fact that we come to church to escape all that worldly, divisive stuff? Yes, we come to church because we want to feel loved and not judged. We come to experience comfort, not challenge. We come to hear the good news of the gospel and not the bad news of the world.

Actually, I find it difficult to preach the prophetic words of scripture. The words of Amos, Isaiah, Jeremiah, Ezekiel, and the words of that most important prophet of all, Jesus — these words do not feel very good. Because they demand personal change, they make us feel guilty. And because they demand social change, they make us feel angry and overwhelmed. Yes, the words about justice in scripture are disturbing. If we preach them, some of us won't like them. If we preach them, maybe then we will have to do them. But the alternative is worse. If we *don't* preach them we are gutting the good news, telling half-truths and sugar-coating the Christian faith.

Despite the fact that the word "justice" feels alien in church, it is a word that appears 83 times in the Old Testament and 34 times in the New Testament. The word "justice" in the Hebrew language literally means rightness — rightness with God and rightness with one another. It is both a means and an end. It is the way we move toward the kingdom of God and it is the shape of the kingdom once we get there. Justice was the vision in the mind of God when the creation was begun and justice was the reality of God when the work of creation was done. Justice was the reality when on the last day God sat back and said, "It is very good."

There are other places in scripture where the word "justice" is not actually used but where its reality is eloquently expressed. Our lesson for this morning is one of those places. Robert McAfee Brown, a Presbyterian theologian, has said that just as the Exodus story is the paradigm for all Hebrew scripture, so this passage from Luke is the paradigm for all of Christian scripture. Today Jesus tells us who he is. He tells us what his purpose is, and by so doing, he tells us what the purpose of the church is.

Luke placed this story where it chronologically does not belong. He placed it at the very beginning of Jesus' ministry, whereas both Mark and Matthew placed it where it actually happened — right before Jesus' death. Luke did this purposely, in order to underline the importance of this event, in order to put a megaphone directly into Jesus' hands, so that we will hear — loudly and clearly — what the Christian life is all about. If Brown is right — that this is the most pivotal passage in the New Testament — then, friends, we have our work cut out for us.

Jesus came back home to crowded, liberal, cosmopolitan Galilee, to the town of Nazareth where he was known as Mary and Joseph's boy. The hometown folk were so glad to see Jesus that they give him the honor of reading scripture in worship — something that any male member of the synagogue would be asked to do. They were very pleased when Jesus chose to read words of promise from Isaiah. These were favorite words about the Messiah and about a time in the future when good news will be preached to the poor, when those in prison will be released, when the blind will be able to see, and when those who are oppressed will be set free. Yes, a time when rightness with God would be established for all — a time when the original justice of creation would be restored.

Now, a couple of things need to be said about this passage. There are innuendos which tell us why Jesus chose these words for Isaiah to form the very first sermon of his career. The word here for "poor" means *poor*, materially poor. When Matthew talks about the poor, he adds "poor in spirit," in order to take some of the economic edge off the words. But Isaiah and Jesus are clear that God's word and God's love must be good news to the poor — those who are experiencing poverty — those who are other than you and me.

The other phrase which Jesus quotes directly from Isaiah is the one that says the Messiah will come "to proclaim the acceptable year of the Lord." It is not just a poetic phrase. It is a religious concept rooted in history and radical in its political and social implications. The acceptable year of the Lord refers to the jubilee year — a social model described in detail in the Hebrew book of Leviticus.

What is a jubilee year? As an act of thanksgiving and an acknowledgement of where all the gifts of life come from, God commands that each fifty years the people of God are to let the soil lie fallow, they are to forgive all debts — that means all material loans — they are to release all the slaves, and most radical of all, they are to redistribute the capital and the land so that everyone has enough and so that no one has too much. This jubilee year — this radical reordering of reality — is what the acceptable year of the Lord means. It is the good news that Isaiah says the Messiah will bring. And it is the scripture which Jesus chose to read in his hometown synagogue when he told the world who he was and what he had come to do.

The reading of this scripture was not the end of what Jesus did that first day of his public ministry. When he finished reading in those mellow, well-modulated tones, with all his articulation in just the right places, he rolled up the scroll, paused dramatically, and then announced that the words of the prophet had come true. They were no longer future words — they were present words. Yes, *he*, the hometown boy, *he*, Jesus of Nazareth, was and is the Messiah — and the work of justice had begun. The jubilee year is *now*, the good news for the poor is *now*, the redistribution of wealth is *now*, the release of the captives and the freedom for all the oppressed is *now*. The new creation of rightness with God for all people — not just the Jews — is *now*. The mission of Jesus and the mission of the church is no more and no more less than the work of justice.

The people of Nazareth didn't want to hear this anymore than we do. They got very angry. Suffice it to say that they were incensed that Jesus would interject harsh demands into the passive comfort of their faith.

This is a story about what it means to be in the right relation with God and with God's people. Yes, it has political implications. It is not a political story but it has political implications for us, about redistributing our taxes in order to bring good news to the poor, and about rethinking our criminal justice system that emphasizes punishment instead of redemption, and about our local budget discussions where the needs of the wealthy are being pitted against the needs of the poor.

There are other places in scripture where this same tension exists. There are places where Jesus does or says things that reflect God's love, and which then lay before us issues of justice. Think about that unnerving parable about the workers in the vineyard where those who labored for eight hours are paid the same as the cripples and drunkards who work for one hour. It is a story that underlines compassion as the heart of God's justice based on what people need instead of what they deserve. And it is a story that has political implications for us when we debate the whole issue of affirmative action.

Think about the story of the woman caught in adultery where all the people are eager to stone her to death as the law required. That is until Jesus intervenes, creating justice by saying: "The one without sin should cast the first stone." Such a spiritual story has definite political overtones when we get to the contemporary story of capital punishment.

And there is Amos, that tree surgeon turned prophet, who tells the appalled people of Israel that God will treat them no better and no worse than everybody else, that being God's special people doesn't give special privileges, it only brings special responsibilities. What does that have to say about current political discussions concerning justice in the Middle East and about the issue of land for Jews and Palestinians?

I could go on and on pulling stories from scripture that seem to talk about love and forgiveness and compassion that have far-reaching implications for our world today. Yes these stories talk about rightness with God and rightness among the people of God. They are stories which talk to us about justice.

Whether it feels good or not, the Bible gives us a justice Jesus and as such, calls us to be a justice church with justice defined as rightness — as a compassionate commitment to creating wholeness and abundance for all. Even though some congregations are uncomfortable having a Justice Committee, we are called to be justice people, righting the wrongs of society and urging our social and political systems to promote rightness with God and with each other.

When Jesus finishes reading the words of Isaiah in the dusty synagogue of Nazareth, he rolls up the scroll and says, "*I* am this Word. *I* am the good news to the poor. *I* am the liberty for the oppressed. *I* am the acceptable year of the Lord. *I* am the justice of God — *my* words, *my* energies, *my* actions, *my* life."

Today when we hear these words from Luke, we as the living Body of Christ are called to respond. We too must close the Bible and say: "*We* are the liberty for the oppressed. *We* are the acceptable year of the Lord. *We* are the justice of God — *our* words, *our* energies, *our* actions, *our* lives."

My friends, it doesn't matter what we name our committees or what name we give to the love of God. All that matters is that we do it.

May it be so for you and for me. Amen.

Epiphany 4
Luke 4:21-30

Then he began to say to them, "Today this scripture has been fulfilled in your hearing." All spoke well of him and were amazed at the gracious words that came from his mouth. They said, "Is not this Joseph's son?" He said to them, "Doubtless you will quote to me this proverb, 'Doctor, cure yourself!' And you will say, 'Do here also in your hometown the things that we have heard you did at Capernaum.' " And he said, "Truly I tell you, no prophet is accepted in the prophet's hometown. But the truth is, there were many widows in Israel in the time of Elijah, when the heaven was shut up three years and six months, and there was a severe famine over all the land; yet Elijah was sent to none of them except to a widow at Zarephath in Sidon. There were also many lepers in Israel in the time of the prophet Elisha, and none of them was cleansed except Naaman the Syrian." When they heard this, all in the synagogue were filled with rage. They got up, drove him out of the town, and led him to the brow of the hill on which their town was built, so that they might hurl him off the cliff. But he passed through the midst of them and went on his way.

Epiphany 4
Luke 4:21-30

How Angry Are You?

I am angry. I am angry that the open-minded, open-hearted denomination I have always loved has become more and more legalistic and polarized. I am angry that my country, the wealthiest and most powerful nation in the world, has one of the highest rates of child mortality and child poverty of any industrialized nation in the world. I am angry that a huge percentage of US foreign aid goes to Israel — one of the richest nations in the world. I am angry that some of those tax dollars are being used to build settlements on confiscated Palestinian land. I am angry that self-righteous terrorists are killing with abandon across the Middle East and around the world. I am angry that most American sports teams and other school activities have become so important and so time intensive that any comprehensive youth program in our congregations seems doomed. I am angry that sometimes in our imperfect world a few of us end up doing more than our share in trying to make this world a more just and healthy place. Yes, I am angry!

But let me reassure you. I'm not angry all of the time. I'm not even angry most of the time, but I am angry some of the time. And unlike a few years ago, I've decided that in some situations, my anger is okay. As the Bible so vividly shows, anger is a normal and necessary human emotion and very often, anger can be a catalyst for transformation, for creativity, and for new life.

The early desert fathers and mothers borrowed a metaphor from Plato and used it to describe the Christian life. They suggested that the human personality is like a chariot pulled by two horses, and driven by a charioteer. The two horses are *anger* and *desire*, and the charioteer is *reason*. Now, in this metaphor, the horses — anger and desire — are understood as the two fundamental drives, or sources of energy, that enable us to live. "Desire" motivates us to draw toward ourselves what we need to live — food, love, shelter. Desire is also a kind of moral instinct that makes us want to be the people God created us to be.

"Anger," on the other hand, is that most primitive drive that empowers us to push ourselves away from danger, discomfort, or pain. Anger is also a kind of moral instinct that identifies obstacles to the good, and provides energy to strive against those obstacles in our desire for a good and whole life of love.

The "chariot" of the Christian life is moving toward a goal, and that goal is the love of God, love of neighbor, and proper love of self. In this metaphor, the charioteer is *reason*. In ideal circumstances, reason is directing, controlling, driving the good energies of anger and desire.

This balanced understanding of anger as part of the creative tension of the moral life helps us to embrace the many stories of Jesus that seem to include his authentic and powerful anger. Harriet Lerner, in her book titled *The Dance of Anger*, defines anger in a positive way as a sign that our needs and wants are not being met, or that our rights or the rights of others are being violated.

Certainly this is how Jesus experienced anger and how he used it. In the gospel of Matthew, we read about Jesus railing at the legalists of his day who were hiding behind the law as an excuse to condone injustice. He rants: "You liars, you hypocrites, you brood of vipers! Repent!" In the gospel of Mark, Jesus is described as "angry" when the Pharisees call him to task for healing on the sabbath. With righteous anger and zeal, Jesus lashes out at their hard-heartedness. On two other occasions, Jesus barks at those closest to him — to his mother and brothers when they interrupt him while he is preaching and to his disciples when they try to keep the little children away from him.

The most famous story of Jesus' anger is the day he marches into the temple and turns over the tax collector's tables, scattering the crowd with his razor sharp whip and excoriating them for their greedy behavior. The fact that these tax collectors are charging exorbitant rates for the doves and lambs required for faithful temple sacrifice simply enrages Jesus. This grab of resources by the privileged 1% at the expense of the poorer 99% causes his rage.

Yes, Jesus sees it as it is and tells it like it is and he uses neither euphemisms nor apologies to blanket his displeasure. Jesus discovers what many psychotherapists have suggested — that healthy anger, honestly expressed, provides needed energy to confront evil and pain and injustice. It seems clear to me that when we talk about the passion of Jesus we need to include more than his suffering, more than his pain, and more than his death. We need to include, recognize, and affirm his anger. We need to welcome our own anger when it seeks, passionately, to affirm life.

That which is a blessing can also be a curse. That which is creative and energizing, can also be dangerous. This certainly is the case with anger. My mother once told me during my adolescent years that my mouth would be the death of me — and others have agreed with her over the years. Quite simply, anger that is uninhibited and undisciplined becomes abusive. Go back to that early Christian metaphor, when the two horses of anger and desire race ahead unbridled by the discipline of reason — the discipline of the charioteer — it is certain that the chariot of life will soon crash in ruins.

Our gospel text for today is another look at the inevitability of anger in our human experience. And this story shows the destructive power of anger. Jesus, freshly baptized and strengthened by his wilderness wrestling match with the devil, comes home to Nazareth. It is here at the very beginning of his public ministry that he preaches his first sermon. The hometown folk are thrilled to hear Joe and Mary's boy proclaim the hope of their Jewish faith. He reads words from Isaiah that conjures up the image of the Messiah who is to come — the one who will preach good news to the poor, who will set free the oppressed, and who will proclaim liberty to the captives.

"Oh, isn't he a fine speaker?" they murmur. "Aren't we proud of our own little Jesus?" That is until he shocks them and offends them. Jesus has the audacity to announce that this mirage of a Messiah is no longer just a future fantasy. "Today," Jesus said, "these words are fulfilled in your hearing. Today this Messiah has come. And that Messiah is me — Jesus — Joe and Mary's boy."

But Jesus does not stop there. "The Messiah," he says, "has not just come to save the Jews but also to save the Gentiles, the foreigner, and the enemy. The Messiah has come to save everyone!"

So offended are these former neighbors and friends, that they run him out of town and they try to throw him off the cliff — three times!

Their anger is simply a cover up for their fear and their self-centeredness. If Jesus is the Messiah — a flesh and blood product of Nazareth — that means they — the ordinary people of an ordinary village — must do the hard work of peace and justice that Jesus describes. And if the promises of salvation are for everyone, then how can that make them — the children of Israel — special?

My friends, when anger is self-centered and fear-focused, it tends to destroy the self and irreparably tear the fabric of community. Frederick Buechner puts it this way:

Of the Seven Deadly Sins, anger is possibly the most fun. To lick your wounds, to smack your lips over grievances long past... is a feast fit for a king. The chief drawback is that what you are wolfing down is yourself.[1]

Yes, selfish anger is sinful anger.

Fortunately, scripture gives us some clues as to how our anger can be disciplined and embraced in holy and life-affirming ways. Step one is basic. We must simply "pay attention to our anger." All those stories about Jesus taking time to get away into the hills, to be alone, to pray, as pious as all that sounds — it is likely that Jesus takes that time to pay attention to his life. He takes time to pay attention to his feelings, to his anger and his fear, to his hopes and to his dreams. Yes, Jesus shows us a way to "befriend" our anger and to accept it as part of who we are, to come to know it and understand it, and then to decide what parts of it are healthy and what parts of it need to be transformed. But such "paying attention" and "befriending" takes time, sometimes alone and sometimes in community, that insures our anger will not become a weapon.

As many congregations across this country face diminishing resources and aging buildings, conflict and anger often emerge out of survival fears. Yes, many churches are recognizing that the thriving congregations of the 1970s and 80s are now smaller, with aging members, and bigger challenges. People with strong opinions and strong convictions often express understandable anxiety through anger — sometimes toward each other, sometimes toward their pastors, and sometimes toward the church at large. To use the metaphor from today's gospel text, there are sometimes efforts to push the ideas and opinions of voices raising difficult issues over the cliff.

Usually, when conflict and disagreement happen, all of us in the fray are participants in the turmoil and the hurt feelings and the raised voices that emerge. We are *all* part of the problem. But, my friends, all of us can also be part of the solution. With intentional and skilled mediation leadership, and with careful listening to brothers and sisters in the faith, any congregation can begin to talk openly about their differences. We can discuss what makes each other angry, about how feelings have been hurt, and how relationships have been damaged. Apologies and fresh promises can emerge. With this kind of strengthened fabric of friendship and community, congregational families can and will move forward into a fresh beginning.

I believe that only this kind of careful "befriending" can turn our anger into a catalyst for change and growth and new life in all areas of our lives. It is only this intentional discipline — this *reason* — that can transform our destructive anger into righteous anger and into a worthy partner with love for pursuing the way and the word of God.

Friends, today Jesus prompts us to recognize both the promise and the peril of anger. All of us are called, as disciples of Jesus Christ, to acknowledge and befriend our own anger so that embracing a discipline of grace we can use the power of our anger to strengthen the church and to heal God's broken world.

May it be so for you and for me. Amen.

---

1. Frederick Buechner, *Wishful Thinking* (New York: Harper and Row, 1973), p. 2.

Epiphany 5
Luke 5:1-11

Once while Jesus was standing beside the lake of Gennesaret, and the crowd was pressing in on him to hear the word of God, he saw two boats there at the shore of the lake; the fishermen had gone out of them and were washing their nets. He got into one of the boats, the one belonging to Simon, and asked him to put out a little way from the shore. Then he sat down and taught the crowds from the boat. When he had finished speaking, he said to Simon, "Put out into the deep water and let down your nets for a catch." Simon answered, "Master, we have worked all night long but have caught nothing. Yet if you say so, I will let down the nets." When they had done this, they caught so many fish that their nets were beginning to break. So they signaled their partners in the other boat to come and help them. And they came and filled both boats, so that they began to sink. But when Simon Peter saw it, he fell down at Jesus' knees, saying, "Go away from me, Lord, for I am a sinful man!" For he and all who were with him were amazed at the catch of fish that they had taken; and so also were James and John, sons of Zebedee, who were partners with Simon. Then Jesus said to Simon, "Do not be afraid; from now on you will be catching people." When they had brought their boats to shore, they left everything and followed him.

Epiphany 5
Luke 5:1-11

Trusting the Other Side

Since her death, Maya Angelou has been greatly celebrated around the world and that is an appropriate response in my mind. Maya was a poet, a prophet, a celebrity, and a grand dame. She was also a lifelong follower of Jesus. Raised in Stamps, Arkansas, by her grandmother, Maya spent much of her childhood within the warm embrace of a small African Methodist Episcopal Church — at least six hours each Sunday according to her own writing. In the last half of her life, she lived in Winston Salem, North Carolina, and was a steadfast member of a black Baptist Church. And yet despite this religious pedigree, Angelou could be very critical of the church. In one of her books, she wrote a rather biting poem titled "Savior," where the poet laments the petulance of priests and the boredom of ritual. She also stresses our need for Jesus to visit us again.

Maya drew a distinction between Jesus and the church. Though we as the church are called to be the resurrected Body of Christ on earth, all too often we substitute institution for incarnation. We have turned Christ's organic body into the static structure of organization. As the established Protestant churches in America continue to diminish and decline, perhaps we can sympathize with Angelou's despair about the vapid tedium of too many of our rituals. And like the poet, we yearn for a fresh visitation from Jesus and a reacquaintance with his holy name.

A few years ago, Leonard Sweet wrote a book called *The Gospel According to Starbucks*. Lifting up Starbucks as one of the capitalist wonders of the modern world, he insists that the church has much to learn from our local coffee hangout. The philosophy of the founder of Starbucks is simple. For him, selling coffee is his *Grand Passion*, except that it is not about coffee. Starbucks is not a coffee shop — it is a lifestyle. It is what Sweet calls "a third place" — a place that every human being needs — a place of comfort and community and connection. It is a place beyond home and work. Church used to be that third place for most Americans, but no more. Instead the music, the techy comfort, the quiet neighborhood hubbub of the local coffee shop has become a place where strangers become friends. And, Sweet suggests, if Jesus showed up tomorrow, he would be more comfortable in Starbucks than in most of our churches.

Riffing off this Starbucks image, I want to agree with Maya Angelou that we need Jesus to visit us again, and we need to recover the radical, rich, and real power that the living Christ offers us inside the church and out. Rather than a bland buddy or pious preacher, the Jesus we meet in scripture is more of a bold barista preparing the unique jolt of spiritual caffeine each of us needs to live our lives fully. And what the church at its best can offer us is not comfort and complacency, but commitment, connection, and conviction. And this is the kind of Jesus we meet in Luke's gospel story for today.

The more I read Luke's account of the calling of the disciples, the more astonished I am at the *chutzpah* Jesus acts out this morning. Here he is, a restless wandering preacher, bored with his father's carpentry shop, and freshly kicked out of town by the neighbors he grew up with. He was kicked out because he proclaimed himself the Messiah — not a Messiah for the chosen few, but a Messiah for all the messy masses. This morning we find him walking by the sea, fending off adoring crowds, looking for a few good people to help him turn the world upside down.

It is important to remember that Simon Peter, James, and John are professional fishermen. They are good at what they do, and they know all the tricks of the trade. Any decent fisherman knows that you never fish close to shore because the only fish stupid enough to flirt with the rocky shore are guppies and tadpoles. Because of the fluid movement of muscle needed to haul in a big catch, the nets are always thrown from one particular side of the boat. When Jesus sees these three brawny, frustrated men coming into shore after a night of nothing, he calls out to them. He tells them to do everything their fishing experience has taught them is wrong — toss their nets into the shallow water from the wrong side of the boat. And according to the text, Peter, John, and James trust Jesus. They obey Jesus. They do what years of training and custom have forbidden them ever to do before.

This electric interaction with Jesus is the only officer training these disciples ever had. They trust and obey. They take a risk. From that moment on they follow Jesus on his Don Quixote quest to catch people for God. Most everything they learn to do while wandering by his side turns conventional wisdom on its ear. Love your enemies, don't hurt them. Focus on the poor, and let the rich fend for themselves. Touch lepers, don't shun them. Invite women into the community of discipleship — don't keep them barefoot and pregnant in the kitchen. Let the little children come, and bless them with all their noise and energy and interruptions. Honor the authority of Caesar, but only give your true allegiance to God. Suffer willingly in order to bring healing to others. And don't be scared of death, for it is only when a seed dies that healthy grain can grow. Not only does Jesus turn fishing wisdom on its ear, he turns living wisdom on its ear. If we want to be disciples of this bold barista of rich, hot, caffeinated faith, then we need to turn the wisdom of our contemporary world on its ear too.

At every transition point in every congregation, it is time to renew our own call to discipleship. No matter how long we have been a good Christian, it may be that Jesus is about to ask us to move beyond our comfort zone. Jesus is about to ask us to "do church" in ways that turn upside down "the way we have always done it." Yes, Jesus is walking along the edge of this community and is calling out to you: "Trust. Trust me. Obey. Obey the radical demands of the gospel. Risk. Risk doing new things in new ways. Cast your nets on the other side of the boat — trusting that fresh grace and abundance will come tumbling into this place."

In trying to infuse the church with the best learning from the Starbucks strategy, Len Sweet has come up with the anagram E-P-I-C. EPIC. He suggests that vital churches in the twenty-first century must be EPIC churches.

E stands for *experiential*. Peter and James and John did not understand discipleship until they did it. We Presbyterians think too much and experience too little. Instead of thinking about prayer, why don't we just pray? Instead of wishing that we had more children in our pews or more people of color in our congregation, why not go out, find them, invite them, and welcome them? Any educator will tell you that children learn by doing, not by listening. Friends let us experience our faith first and then we will discover what we really believe.

P stands for *participatory*. There is no way that Peter could have hauled in all those fish by himself. He needed the other men in his boat to help him — and even then with all of them pulling with all their might — they barely managed to capture all that abundance.

One good trend in Presbyterian worship is the rise in participation of all the people in the pews. As Kierkegaard so aptly suggested in Christian worship the "audience" is

God — and we — you and I — are the actors. We are all playing the various parts in acting out the drama of scripture. Rather than listening to a concert, we are all called to make music — to sing, to clap occasionally, and to feel the gospel in our bones and our blood. More and more of our churches are encouraging weekly communion and often by intinction. People actually getting up and walking forward encourages offering ourselves to God as we are fed with the Bread of Life and the Cup of Blessing. And in growing family congregations, children are more and more an active part of worship participating in the liturgy, and not just restlessly waiting to be released for Sunday school.

Recently, I was at the Beacon Church for worship. Seven years ago, they had almost no children. Today, they have dozens, and twenty of them were in worship in the middle of August — in a congregation of 125 adult members. Some of the children wandered around during the scripture and the hymns. As a group they led The Lord's Prayer, they poured water into the Baptismal font during the Assurance of Pardon, and they played raucous instruments during the Doxology. Despite occasional noise and motion, not one older member seemed to mind. Friends, if we participate — if each one of has a chance to act out the various parts of worship — then it becomes part of our bodies and our souls and not just passive entertainment for our minds.

I stands for *image rich*. Images, metaphors, stories, visual art, banners, colors, water, bread, wine, instruments, dance, poetry, video clips are welcome. More and more worship and education is becoming a goldmine for the senses and the imagination. After all, God cannot be fully captured by words or doctrines. Jesus is a person, not an idea and the more we play with images, the more the Spirit can fertilize our hearts.

Finally, *C* is for *connection*. This is not just the "friendly" connections at coffee hour but the more intimate connections of heart-to-heart relationships and of taking off our masks. This is the connection of trusting that our brothers and sisters in Christ want to really know us and that we can trust both our joys and our sorrow, our successes and our failures into each other's keeping. In addition, a truly connected church is one who is not just bound together with those inside these walls but also bound together with the people outside these walls — our neighbors, those who are different, and those who are in need.

One of the enduring images for me from the tumultuous week in Ferguson, Missouri, was the picture of 100 volunteers from five local churches who banded together to reach out to their community. The morning after the first night of rioting, they arrived outside the looted stores to clean up the glass, to reach out to the protestors, and to get to know their neighbors. They made a connection with strangers in order to become friends.

So, there you have it. EPIC — experiential, participatory, image-rich, and connected — a caffeinated, committed, community of disciples — trusting, obeying, risking — all to the glory of God. Dear friends, this is my dream for you, my prayer for you, as you move forward on your journey as Christ's people. To paraphrase a blessing I received on my wedding day almost forty years ago: May your life together be as comfortable as an old shoe, and as mysterious as a Chinese puzzle.

May it be so. Amen.

Epiphany 6
Luke 6:17-26

He came down with them and stood on a level place, with a great crowd of his disciples and a great multitude of people from all Judea, Jerusalem, and the coast of Tyre and Sidon. They had come to hear him and to be healed of their diseases; and those who were troubled with unclean spirits were cured. And all in the crowd were trying to touch him, for power came out from him and healed all of them. Then he looked up at his disciples and said: "Blessed are you who are poor, for yours is the kingdom of God. Blessed are you who are hungry now, for you will be filled. Blessed are you who weep now, for you will laugh. Blessed are you when people hate you, and when they exclude you, revile you, and defame you on account of the Son of Man. Rejoice in that day and leap for joy, for surely your reward is great in heaven; for that is what their ancestors did to the prophets. But woe to you who are rich, for you have received your consolation. Woe to you who are full now, for you will be hungry. Woe to you who are laughing now, for you will mourn and weep. Woe to you when all speak well of you, for that is what their ancestors did to the false prophets."

EPIPHANY 6
LUKE 6:17-26

HOLY HAPPINESS

Psychiatrist Robert Coles tells a story about a poor black woman in New Orleans who sells her body almost every night to wealthy old men in order to take care of her five children. And each night this woman takes half of what she earns as a prostitute and gives it to the nuns who run the local soup kitchen. Coles asks the question, "Is this woman blessed or is she cursed?" From her perspective, I'm sure the answer is both. But from the perspective of today's gospel lesson, she is more blessed than she is cursed.

The entire spectrum of biblical scholars — from conservative to liberal — agree that the words of the Beatitudes form the very core of Jesus' ministry. Yes, these no-nonsense words give to us his central wisdom, his focused vision, and his principle mandate.

Both the gospel of Luke and the gospel of Matthew record the words of the Beatitudes. But there are major differences in the two presentations. Matthew has Jesus leaving the crowd and going up a mountain away from the hubbub to share these words with just a few chosen disciples. Luke, on the other hand, has Jesus coming down the mountain, onto the plain, where the crowds surge around him, trying to touch him. They are trying to literally suck into themselves the power coming out of him. Matthew has nine blessings. Luke has four. Matthew "spiritualizes" the beatitudes — blessed are the "poor in spirit." Luke is much more blunt. "Blessed are the poor" — period. Matthew puts it all in the third person — blessed are "those." Luke brings the words home — blessed are you — right here in the present. Finally, Matthew keeps things on a positive note — focusing only on blessings. Luke matches the blessings with an equal number of curses. Yes, Luke reminds us that the opposite of blessing is woe and for God, both/and not either/or is the way things are.

As is the custom in many worshiping communities, many of you responded to today's gospel lesson: "This is the word of the Lord. Thanks be to God." But did you — do we — really mean that? Are we truly thankful for these words from Luke? In his straightforward way Jesus tells us that those who are blessed, those who are "happy" according to another translation, are the poor, the hungry, the ones who are weeping. Blessed are those who are hated and excluded. And then to make matters worse, he says, "Woe to you who are rich. Woe to you who are full. Woe to you who are laughing. Cursed are you who enjoy the admiration of others." Friends, no matter which way we slice it, we are in the cursed group and not the blessed group, at least much of the time. Indeed, as *The Message* by Eugene Peterson suggests: "Some of you are rich, too bad for you; you have had all you will get." What is going on here?

There is a true story about a Quaker who put up a sign on the vacant piece of land next to his house. It read: This Land Will Be Given To Anyone Who Is Truly Satisfied. A wealthy farmer who was riding by stopped to read the sign and said to himself, "Since I have all I need as a wealthy man, I certainly qualify. I might as well claim the land."

He approached the Quaker to seal the deal. "And art thou truly satisfied?" the Quaker inquired.

"I am, indeed. I have all that I need."

"Friend," said the Quaker, "if thou art satisfied, what dost thou want the land for?"

What does it take to make us satisfied? What does it take to make us "happy"? And is happiness the same as blessing? In his book *Making Sense of Suffering*, Peter Kreeft suggests that the modern *summum bonum* is pleasure, control, and conquering suffering. Yes, the modern drive is to pit human power over against nature and to see suffering as scandal, and to rise above it at all costs. He goes on to remind us that the *summum bonum* of the Christian life is very different. It is to glorify God and to enjoy God forever — and sometimes that means entering and embracing a world full of suffering. In other words, happiness is not a warm puppy — it is not about feeling good but about *being* good. Blessedness is not about the "good life." It is about a life that is good.

The Hebrew writers have given us a very simple image this morning to understand the tension between "happiness" as the world defines it and "happiness" as God offers it. It is the image of a tree planted by streams of living water so deeply rooted in the ways of God that no matter how violent or desolate the world around us may become, we stay connected in a very deep and basic way — connected to the vast oceans of God's grace.

Several years ago, when some of us visited the Middle East, we were struck by the vivid difference between Galilee — the verdant, green, watered haven in the north of Palestine versus the Dead Sea region — the vast stretch of desolation, knee deep in barren salt, just a hundred miles south of Nazareth. The aquamarine sparkle of that water is dazzling with a kind of deathly beauty. But it is a no man's land where the glaring sun and parched earth destroy any inkling of life close by.

This morning, when Jeremiah compares a shrub in the uninhabited salt land with a tree planted by water he is literally giving us a choice between life and death. Do we trust the dazzling desert of the world's ways or do we trust the rich soil of God, constantly being fed by streams of living water? The choice is ours, but the consequences are clear. Rooted only in the ways of the world, we will quickly shrivel up and die. But rooted in the moist promises of God, we — in the words of the prophet — "shall not fear when the heat comes," and "in the year of the drought, we will not be anxious" and "our leaves will stay green and our branches will bear fruit."

I think Jesus is saying two things to us today. First of all, he is saying that when we live out of vulnerability and need — out of our emptiness and not out of our fullness — it is then that we can connect with God and that God can give us what we need. Jesus is not saying that it is bad to be rich or full, to be healthy, strong, or lighthearted. Rather he is suggesting that fullness and satisfaction lead to self-sufficiency and self-absorption — a state of independence that distances us from God and leads us to glorify ourselves instead of the holy one who has given us life.

For several years, during my early thirties, I stopped crying. I don't know exactly why but it may have had something to do with control and climbing the ladder and trying to "make it" in the professional world. I didn't have time to think about sadness, injustice, suffering, or vulnerability. I was just too busy creating success in my life. And yet I remember feeling sad from time to time, sad, because I couldn't muster the tears. I couldn't access my feelings and I had lost the ability to be vulnerable. I felt very far away from God. These days, tears come frequently and easily to me as much in times of joy as in times of sorrow. And often my tears flow for the pain of others, not just for myself. I certainly don't feel as "in control" as I used to. But I do feel more human, much more connected to and dependent upon God. Life is somehow much richer. Yes, I understand why Jesus says "Blessed are those who weep."

This past couple of weeks there have been a lot of tears flowing around here. Some of you are watching a beloved parent die and the pain is excruciating, so the tears flow. Some of you are facing your own mortality because of serious disease and tears of fear, rage, and sadness often threaten to drown you.

I am always somewhat surprised when people apologize to me for crying or seem embarrassed by their tears. Friends, I believe that our weeping is a gift. Our tears soften the suffering of the human condition. In a strange way, they connect us deeply with the mysteries of life and death. What Jesus is offering us today, what Jesus is inviting us to experience today, is the rich honesty of vulnerability and the deep soil of our own human need. And what Jesus promises is the nourishment of mercy and healing that God gives to us when we are rooted in the holy.

Our scripture goes on to give us a second even stronger message. Not only are we called to recognize our own need and dependence upon God. We are called to recognize the need and vulnerability of others. And then to offer to them, through our lives, the rich soil of compassion and justice. We are called to be in solidarity with the poor, the hungry, with those who are weeping. We are called to be part of the solution and not part of the problem. Biblical scholars point out that the Beatitudes are what is called a "performative word." These predictions about blessedness are not *going* to happen — they are already happening. This is not about what might be. This is about what is. This is God's agenda, God's vision, God's kingdom. The reality described by the Beatitudes will happen, is happening, whether we choose to be part of it or not. Only a few of us are called to *be* the poor. A few more of us are called to work *with* the poor. But *all* of us are called to be *for* the poor — because that's what it means to be God's people.

My friends, our scripture readings for today remind us that "human happiness" and "holy happiness" are often two different kinds of reality. Jesus is suggesting that "blessing" is more than enjoying ourselves. The goal of life is more than self-fulfillment. And prosperity is more than getting what we want. Happiness is to be open to God. Blessedness is to be fully alive and in harmony with God's ways both in the good times and the bad. Let us be comforted and instructed by the words of the psalmist:

> *Happy are those who delight in the Lord. They are like trees planted by streams of water, which yield their fruit in its season, and their leaves do not wither. In all that they do, they prosper.*
> (Psalm 1)

May it be so for you and for me. Amen.

Epiphany 7
Luke 6:27-38

But I say to you that listen, love your enemies, do good to those who hate you, bless those who curse you, pray for those who abuse you. If anyone strikes you on the cheek, offer the other also; and from anyone who takes away your coat do not withhold even your shirt. Give to everyone who begs from you; and if anyone takes away your goods, do not ask for them again. Do to others as you would have them do to you. If you love those who love you, what credit is that to you? For even sinners love those who love them. If you do good to those who do good to you, what credit is that to you? For even sinners do the same. If you lend to those from whom you hope to receive, what credit is that to you? Even sinners lend to sinners, to receive as much again. But love your enemies, do good, and lend, expecting nothing in return. Your reward will be great, and you will be children of the most high; for he is kind to the ungrateful and the wicked. Be merciful, just as your Father is merciful. Do not judge, and you will not be judged; do not condemn, and you will not be condemned. Forgive, and you will be forgiven; give, and it will be given to you. A good measure, pressed down, shaken together, running over, will be put into your lap; for the measure you give will be the measure you get back.

Epiphany 7
Luke 6:27-38

God's Absurd Answer

In a stunning biblical slap in the face, our gospel reading for this morning also served as the lectionary text ten days after 9/11 — ten days after Ground Zero became a devastating reality in our nation's history. Love our enemies? Offer forgiveness? God, you have to be kidding!

That first week after 9/11 — after the terror struck — after our world changed forever — I kept reading about other ministers who were preaching about forgiveness. "How can they do that?" I asked myself. You see, I simply was not there. At that point, all I could do was grieve, cry, and worry — and rage in aimless ways at the monsters who did this. Now, years later, with feelings more modulated, with a nation transformed and reshaped in a way we could not have imagined, and with the shadows of terrorism still assaulting our world, I find myself drawn to the impossible teachings of our faith. In Luke's ancient words, and with God's sobering wisdom, we are being called to figure out what forgiveness and what loving our enemies means. We are called to figure what it means today, while bodies are still being blown up all over the world.

It is an ugly thing when religion turns violent, and it is a sad thing. God is twisted into a grotesque caricature — a demagogue feeding the bloodthirsty anger of narrow minds — a cosmic fanatic creating human fanatics here on earth. Fanatical Christians roaming around abortion clinics and calling homosexuals demeaning names. Fanatical Jews pulverizing Palestinian homes built on land owned by Arabs for generations and killing children who are only throwing rocks. Fanatical Muslims using innocent passengers as ammunition for horrendous death, killing teenagers in Jerusalem, and teaching their children to hate Jews and destroy Israel. Isn't it strange that the three world religions who claim Abraham as their father should all have the same problem? All three religions have spawned ideological fanatics who have somehow forgotten that according to scripture, Abraham was not allowed to kill Isaac? Why? Because a good and gracious God intervened.

It's so easy to decide that as Christians we are better than the Muslims or Jews. After all, they keep waging "holy war" and proclaiming that God vanquishes evil through the sacrifice of soldiers and martyrs. But my friends, sit down and read the Old Testament. Sit down and read the Passion Story in the New Testament and you will find enough blood and guts to last you a lifetime. Chapter after chapter in Kings and Judges, in the prophets and the psalms talk about God slaughtering the enemy through the bravery of the Israelites — tens of thousands at a time. And then there is that awful verse in Psalm 137 when the exiled people of God are lamenting their devastating lives and they dream about revenge. They dream about how happy they will be when they take the babies of their enemies and dash them against the rock. Quite simply in all religious history there is a wide spectrum of human emotion and action. Again and again, we see "holy" scripture being used to feed human hatred. Because God is often described through the perspective and experience of sinful people, we find primitive and partial interpretations of God portraying the holy one as bloody and violent.

And yet we are learning that violence is not the main message of the Koran. Nor is it the main lesson of the Bible. In many of the psalms, in the lyric poetry of Isaiah, in the patient wisdom of Job, in the stories of Moses, David, Hannah, and Miriam, and in the earth-shattering story of Jesus, we meet a different God. We meet a more mature God who refuses to let death ever be the answer for life. If we get stuck in the primitive, violent portraits of God we will be primitive and violent in our contemporary actions. But if we look at the whole biblical story and if we accept the moral and historic evolution of God and God's people, we will learn different ways of responding to the evil in our world. The foundation of the Christian answer to evil, hatred, violence, and unspeakable destruction is — believe it or not — love and forgiveness, reconciliation and restoration. It is a resurrected sense of human community arising out of the fragmented ashes of a violent world. Yes, according to our crucified and resurrected Lord, the best way to honor those who have been destroyed through war and terrorism is to love our enemies, do good to those who hate us, bless those who curse us, to refrain from judgment and retaliation, and to honor the dead by refusing to hate or abuse those who killed them. It isn't easy to be a follower of Jesus.

Friends, as we look back over the last fifteen years, it is clear that we are still struggling to live out a Christian response to the violence and evil that exploded on 9/11. Though our military strength has routed out the leaders of Al Queda, the cost of two wars has ripped the fabric of our national life to shreds. Though there is more interfaith conversation and exploration than ever before, we still see fear and misunderstanding of our Muslim and Jewish neighbors restricting the fullness of our lives. And in the midst of major economic, political, and environmental crises, we are pulling apart rather than working together as the universal family of God's people. Perhaps the best way we can remember the victims of irrational terrorism is to recommit ourselves to model a different way of living — to be merciful as God in heaven is merciful — to do the hard work of reconciliation, re-creation, and resurrection in a world still steeped in death. We need to do this not just as citizens on a national level, but as Christians on a local level.

Within our contemporary Protestant American world, conflict, anger, and tension is causing deep divisions within the Body of Christ. In the Presbyterian church, our thirty-year struggle to understand and fully welcome the gay and lesbian community has led to the departure of dozens of congregations and incensed brothers and sisters who can't believe that gay ordination and gay marriage is now a choice for those pastors, sessions, and congregations who understand God's grace to be all inclusive. How can Presbyterians read the same scripture in two such opposite ways? How can we interpret sin so differently? The financial and emotional brokenness that these decisions have brought about has torn asunder the Christian community. But, my friends, disruption, conflict, and confusion are nothing new within the Christian church — starting with those early followers of Jesus.

Jesus' words this morning confront us in the midst of our divisions, suspicions, and brokenness. In his most famous sermon, Jesus beseeches us to: "love our enemies, do good to those who hate us... pray for those who abuse us... be merciful as our Father in heaven is merciful." My friends, let us remember what "love" means in the New Testament. It does not mean affection, respect, or a warm, fuzzy feeling. No, in the gospel of Jesus Christ, love — *agape* — is a moral choice. It is an act of the will. It is the resolute and gut-based decision to will and wish the best for the other no matter what. Love is the decision to find the image of God in our enemy and respond gracefully to that image for the sake of God and for the sake of life. And whether we like it or not, whether we understand it or not, love and forgiveness are God's absurd answer to the devastation of these days.

Two contrasting experiences in my own life have helped me understand the difference today's gospel lesson can make.

In the mid 1990s — in between the First and Second Intifada in Israel/Palestine — I took a trip to the Holy Land with a small group of Christians. We worked through the Middle East Council of Churches to set up a balanced trip, with a Palestinian Christian as our guide. We visited Yad Vashem, the Holocaust Museum in Jerusalem then talked with leaders of a Jewish settlement and with leaders from the Knesset. The second half of the trip we traveled through the West Bank, living with Palestinian Christians and visiting unrecognized villages where Palestinian homes and olive groves had been illegally destroyed by Israeli soldiers. It saddened our small group to see the mutual hatred and anger brewing between these two peoples.

One day we went to Hebron and visited a holy site that is sacred to both Muslims and Jews — one half of the sanctuary has become a mosque and the other half is a Jewish synagogue. Our Arab guide went to speak to the Israeli soldier guarding the entrance to the synagogue in order to gain entry to the space. Soon an argument broke out between the two of them as the soldier resisted our visit, distrusting our Palestinian guide. As they shouted at each other with bitter anger in their voices, I couldn't help notice that with their dark Semitic hair and skin, these two "enemies" looked like twins. In a modern twist on the Cain and Abel story, I began to understand how so much hatred had grown between two peoples who are so much alike.

However, a contrasting experience ten years later has given me some hope. Several years after 9/11, I attended an interfaith peace conference in Washington DC. It began with a powerful worship service that involved the participation of Muslims, Christians, and Jews. The service concluded with a candle lighting ritual. The mother of one of the 9/11 terrorists and the mother of one of the 9/11 victims stood side by side and read a litany of forgiveness and peace. Then each of them took an individual lighted candle and together lit one central candle — a clear sign that life is victorious over death and love is victorious over hate.

Following Jesus is difficult and asks us to take our deepest emotions and put them at the service of God's mercy and love. The good news of Jesus Christ is often hard news. Friends, let us believe and may God help our unbelief.

May it be so. Amen.

Epiphany 8
Luke 6:39-49

He also told them a parable: "Can a blind person guide a blind person? Will not both fall into a pit? A disciple is not above the teacher, but everyone who is fully qualified will be like the teacher. Why do you see the speck in your neighbor's eye, but do not notice the log in your own eye? Or how can you say to your neighbor, 'Friend, let me take out the speck in your eye,' when you yourself do not see the log in your own eye? You hypocrite, first take the log out of your own eye, and then you will see clearly to take the speck out of your neighbor's eye. No good tree bears bad fruit, nor again does a bad tree bear good fruit; for each tree is known by its own fruit. Figs are not gathered from thorns, nor are grapes picked from a bramble bush. The good person out of the good treasure of the heart produces good, and the evil person out of evil treasure produces evil; for it is out of the abundance of the heart that the mouth speaks. Why do you call me 'Lord, Lord,' and do not do what I tell you? I will show you what someone is like who comes to me, hears my words, and acts on them. That one is like a man building a house, who dug deeply and laid the foundation on rock; when a flood arose, the river burst against that house but could not shake it, because it had been well built. But the one who hears and does not act is like a man who built a house on the ground without a foundation. When the river burst against it, immediately it fell, and great was the ruin of that house."

EPIPHANY 8
LUKE 6:39-49

IT'S NOT ABOUT ME

In forty years of ordained ministry, I have never preached on this morning's gospel text, which is a pretty good indication that I have been avoiding it. I have discovered over the years that the texts I ignore are the very ones that most describe me. And when it comes to specks and logs, I am an expert. But then most of us are.

These three parables at the end of Luke 6 are the very end of Jesus' sermon on the plain — Luke's version of the Sermon on the Mount. As you may remember in Matthew, Jesus' most famous sermon takes place on a mountain far away from the crowd — hard and demanding words for just a few — the inner circle — the chosen twelve. But in Luke, this very same sermon is preached down on the plain in the midst of the crowds with equally hard and demanding words but meant for all of us who through the ages have tried to follow Jesus. And what Luke reminds us is that though the *call* of discipleship is pure gift and pure grace from God, the *life* of discipleship is hard work. *Being* Christian demands *doing* Christian — bearing good fruit, building strong foundations — and most of all connecting with people around us — whether we like them or not.

At the summer Presbytery Gathering at Camp Holmes, we began with open space conversation groups — discussion groups spontaneously created on the spot. About 20 of the 120 people gathered chose to pull their chairs together and talk about conflict in the church — specifically the vast difference of opinion that has occurred in some congregations following the PCUSA General Assembly in Detroit this past June. As you may know, this year's General Assembly made the *New York Times* twice in one week. Not only did the 650 elected commissioners vote to make gay marriage an option, but this Assembly also voted to divest in three corporations whose products are used by Israel to carry out the occupation in the Palestinian territories. The gay marriage option passed by a two to one margin but the divestment vote was breathtakingly close — 310 to 303. And lest some of you are upset about either of these votes, rest assured that you don't have to agree with them. The General Assembly speaks *to* the church, not *for* the church, so these public stances are guidance, not law. And yet, in a representative democracy, the majority gets to speak no matter how close the vote.

As is always the case, decisions made at this and other General Assemblies have caused a fallout across the church. In an open conversation, one of our pastors talked about the angry threats that some of his parishioners made following the gay marriage vote — threats to withhold money, threats to split the church, threats to leave. He was asking for wisdom from the other elders and pastors gathered about how to respond to the anger, to the judgment, and to the pain that he was hearing from some of his people.

The next 45 minutes were fascinating and very healing. A variety of folks talked about conflict and differences in their congregations and about how hard it is to be the church when people disagree. The consensus that emerged was that we are not called to agree and we are not called to be all alike. In fact, the very nature of the Body of Christ is diversity — diversity of opinion, diversity of gifts, diversity of identity. Unity is not about uniformity, but about covenant faithfulness to the same Lord we all serve. What makes the church the church is listening, hearing, understanding, and accepting — not judging, arguing, or insisting on our own way. In other words, in the church it is not about me — it is about *we*.

The pastor who started the conversation was encouraged to reach out and listen to the anger and the pain, but not to allow one or two angry voices to absorb all his attention or take up all of his time. Instead, differences about gay marriage, gun control, abortion, divestment, or whatever issue sparks controversy — these differences provide an opportunity, rather than a threat. These difficult moments offer an opportunity for education, an opportunity for conversation, and an opportunity for everyone to grow bigger in spirit by listening and learning from one another.

That brings us to specks and logs. Just before our morning verses in Luke we hear Jesus say: "Do not judge, and you will not be judged; do not condemn, and you will not be condemned... for the measure you give will be the measure you get back" (vv. 37, 38b). And then to illustrate, he talks about specks and logs: "Why do you see the speck in your neighbor's eye, but do not notice the log in your own?" (v. 41).

In other words, friends, if you are like me the judgments we make about others are often totally obscured by our own prejudices, our own fears, and our own logs. Most likely, when we are particularly vehement in our judgment of others, we are avoiding a similar vice or fault in ourselves.

How often do we see a smug politician condemning others for sexual immorality, only to discover that this same politician is having a secret affair? How many anti-homosexual activists are secretly afraid that they, or one of their children, are gay? Or how many parents judge their adult children for behaviors or values that they secretly despise in themselves? The apple seldom falls far from the tree. As one writer puts it. "The problem is not other people. The problem is people — and I am one of those people." We are all part of the problem, and we all need to be part of the solution.

The situation unfolding in Israel and Gaza just becomes more horrifying by the day. And this is the third time in eight years that Arabs and Jews have destroyed each other in that tiny strip of arid land on the Mediterranean coast. Thousands of years of hatred and religious strife and geographic rivalry have planted huge logs in the eyes of the Israelis and in the eyes of Hamas. And yet their feelings, needs, and fears are the same — as is their yearning for security in a land of their own, with freedom and prosperity and a future for their families. And yet the death toll just continues to grow. The vast majority of them are innocent civilians and a horrifying number of them children. The conflict is so bitter and the hatred is so deep that any chance of resolution seems impossible. And it is impossible as long as each side fixates on the speck in the other side's eyes instead of taking the enormous logs out of their own.

What the Middle East needs and what our contentious congregations need is a good dose of Jesus. It is what bickering families need. It is what we all need. Not a doctrinal — I'm saved and your not — Jesus, but the earthy, tough, transforming Jesus we hear about today. The unique power of the Christian faith is not *what* we do but *how* we do it. The teachings of Jesus offer an alternative vision and a countercultural ethic that turns conventional wisdom on its ear. Not war, but peace. Not judgment, but respect. Not one-upmanship, but community. Not either/or — either my way or your way — but both/and — a third way that respects our differences and embraces our diversity. We need a new way that loves enemies, endures pain, and transforms suffering — a both/and way that creates a world together that is better than anyone of us can create alone.

Several years ago, the two Presbyterian churches in Middletown, New York, faced a tough decision. Located one block from each other, both churches were struggling with aging buildings, diminishing resources, and older memberships. It slowly dawned on them that two churches so close together made no sense, and their struggles to survive were preventing each congregation from serving the needs of their impoverished neighborhood. With presbytery help, they muddled through five years of joint Session meetings, joint planning, and joint worship but neither of them wanted to give up their building. Finally, they voted to merge without resolving the building issue. They just kept struggling with bills they could not pay.

And then, in a moment of courage and wisdom, the new Session took a leap of faith. They voted to put both buildings on the market and give up the building that sold first. By removing logs of judgment about those "other" people, they became clear eyed enough to see a vision of re-energized ministry within the community around them. It was a vision realizing that flesh and blood was more important than bricks and mortar.

The newer of the two buildings was eagerly purchased by a thriving Latino-Pentecostal congregation. The older building has been spruced up and become home to a blended congregation of renewed Presbyterians, who have learned to love each other. But much more importantly, their newly opened Thrift Shop and Food Pantry is transforming the neighborhood around the church. Conflict has been transformed into community, and judgment has been transformed into justice and joy. Thanks be to God!

A few years ago, I heard one of our Presbyterian mission workers tell a story about his work in Africa. He was serving in a sub-Saharan country that was in conflict with one of its neighbors. The fight, as it usually is, was over land, resources, and tribal rivalries that pitted one country against the other. This mission worker remembered one particularly violent clash where soldiers and rebels were massacring each other in growing numbers. But in the midst of it all, there was a tableau of peace and understanding, of human contact and human love.

At the border of these two countries a small number of mothers from each rival nation were standing, facing each other through a crude fence. As gunfire erupted all around them, these mothers were quietly passing their babies through the fence, and they were nursing each other's children. Somehow, these women were able to take the logs out of their own eyes and see the specks of light in their enemy's eyes. And with the very milk of kindness they were nourishing hope for their children's future.

Friends in Christ, with God's help and with a strong foundation of community and gospel values, we Jesus people are called to bear rich fruit in our communities and around the world. Let us continue to clean out the specks and logs from our eyes so that the light of Christ can be seen clearly in who we are and what we do.

May it be so. Amen.

Epiphany 9
Luke 7:1-10

After Jesus had finished all his sayings in the hearing of the people, he entered Capernaum. A centurion there had a slave whom he valued highly, and who was ill and close to death. When he heard about Jesus, he sent some Jewish elders to him, asking him to come and heal his slave. When they came to Jesus, they appealed to him earnestly, saying, "He is worthy of having you do this for him, for he loves our people, and it is he who built our synagogue for us." And Jesus went with them, but when he was not far from the house, the centurion sent friends to say to him, "Lord, do not trouble yourself, for I am not worthy to have you come under my roof; therefore I did not presume to come to you. But only speak the word, and let my servant be healed. For I also am a man set under authority, with soldiers under me; and I say to one, 'Go,' and he goes, and to another, 'Come,' and he comes, and to my slave, 'Do this,' and the slave does it." When Jesus heard this he was amazed at him, and turning to the crowd that followed him, he said, "I tell you, not even in Israel have I found such faith." When those who had been sent returned to the house, they found the slave in good health.

Epiphany 9
Luke 7:1-10

Trusting Authority

I want to tell you three stories about three men who wrestled with the authority of Jesus. And none of them met Jesus until they had first achieved phenomenal success in the secular world.

Story One

Sam showed up in worship after he married Cheryl, a lifelong member of the congregation. He had been raised as a secular Jew, and when I met him he was a curious agnostic — eager to argue and debate the fine points of theology. The congregation I was serving has shared space with a Jewish synagogue for over fifty years. Sam joined the Bethesda Jewish Congregation while he continued to worship with us every Sunday morning. When Lucy was born, Cheryl and Sam were faced with the decision every interfaith couple has to make — which community of faith would become their daughter's spiritual home? Meanwhile, Sam started attending all our adult education seminars and Bible studies, chewing on the faith with great appetite and relish. One day, he called me — wanting to come in and talk with me.

I think I knew what was coming, and I dreaded it. The last thing I wanted to communicate to our trusted Jewish friends down the hall was that we were eager to convert their flock. But when Sam sat down and told me he was ready to be baptized, the tears in his eyes and the passion in his heart could not be denied. He still did not "understand" the gospel teachings. He still did not "believe" all the tenets of Christian doctrine. All he knew was that he loved and trusted Jesus and the spiritual authority of this radical, first-century rabbi had become the center of his life.

A month later, Sam knelt in front of 300 people and received the lavish blessing of baptism, one year after Lucy had been baptized on the same spot. All of us present that day had a sense that Sam had come home, and he had something to teach the rest of us about submitting to the authority, the lordship of Jesus Christ. The Jewish rabbi from our sister congregation sent me a letter asking that I read it during the baptismal service. He congratulated Sam on his spiritual courage. He invited him to continue his friendship with the Jewish congregation, and he offered him rich blessings as his spiritual journey continued to unfold.

Story Two

The centurion we meet this morning in Luke's gospel is a man who well understands the power and the responsibility of authority. He is a commander in the Roman army and he expects and receives the allegiance and obedience of the soldiers under his command. It also appears that although he is a Gentile, he is a friend of the Jews, enjoying their worship, respecting their ethical teachings, and supporting the local community by financing their synagogue. Like Sam, he is a seeker, but not quite yet a believer.

At first glance we may consider this particular gospel account to be a healing story. But the healing is secondary to the trust that this centurion has for a rabbi he has never met. According to the cultural norms of that day, the centurion has more professional authority than this wandering rabbi. But from all that the centurion has heard, from the stories of all the people who have been healed and transformed by Jesus, this Roman soldier trusts the authority of Jesus more than his own. He sends Jesus a message, begging him to come and heal a much loved servant. Impressed by such blind trust, Jesus sets off for the centurion's house only to be stopped by another messenger. The centurion is so confident in Jesus' power to heal that he says: "You do not need to come to my house. Just speak the word and I know that my servant will be healed." My friends, the faith which Jesus instills in this stranger is nothing more and nothing less than the confidence and trust that the centurion has in the authority of Jesus.

Story Three

Matsui was a brilliant physicist doing esoteric research down the street at the National Institutes of Health. He also worshiped in our pews every Sunday with his wife, Suzuki, and their son, Matsui Jr. Both husband and wife were scientists and immigrants-turned-citizens from Japan. Suzuki was a baptized Christian — one of the 2% of Japanese nationals who choose to be Christian in a country dominated by atheists, Buddhists, and followers of Shinto. Matsui was raised in a home with a Shinto shrine but it was more about ritual and appeasing the gods than providing a deep sense of connection and purpose in life. Yet despite this background, there Matsui sat every week being a good father to his son. He would lean forward and listen more intently to the scripture and the sermon than anyone else in the congregation.

Finally one day, I found the courage to stop Matsui at the door and I asked if he would like to sit down and talk about his faith and about the church. He was somewhat startled, but agreed. A week later we met in my study. He told me his story. In just the past few months he had started having vivid dreams and they were all about Jesus. As a child in Japan, he went to a school run by Catholic nuns, and he had learned about the crucifixion and about how Jesus had to suffer and die for human sin. The nuns had instilled in Matsui a deep sense of unworthiness — that nothing could atone for his imperfections except the bloody sacrifice of the cross. As an adult, Matsui kept having dreams about the crucifixion — dark, scary, violent dreams about sin and death and his own unworthiness. But one night, the dream changed and Matsui saw a kind and gentle Jesus hanging on the cross, but bathed in golden light. This luminous Jesus was looking straight at Matsui with love, and in the dream, Jesus reached out to him and embraced him.

As Matsui told me this story, we both cried. His finely honed scientific mind still resisted much of Christian doctrine, but his heart told him that Jesus lives. More specifically he knew that Jesus lives in Matsui. For the first time in his life he felt accepted and loved unconditionally. Matsui was baptized with his son a few weeks later and in that moment, the life of the congregation changed.

When the congregation decided to have a showing of art created by church members, Matsui brought in two huge oil canvases — one of a dark, bleeding Jesus, and one of a bright, loving Jesus. Matsui, like Sam, like the centurion, and like some of us, encountered a living Christ, and he willingly and joyfully submitted to the lordship of Jesus in his life.

My call to ministry emerged in the midst of the second wave of feminism, and I, like many young women in my generation, was eager to confront sexism and gain credibility and authority in my chosen profession. But there was — and is — a problem with all of this. Ministry is all about servanthood. Ministry is all about serving the needs of others. Ministry is all about submitting to the power and authority of God as well as submitting to the power and authority of the church. Needless to say, I have had struggles with this dichotomy between servanthood and authority for all of my forty years as a pastor.

I remember going to a retreat for clergywomen when I was in my early thirties. A feminist biblical scholar was the retreat leader, and she led us through a journey of re-interpreting some of the pivotal stories of scripture. Miriam is as important to the liberation of the Israelites as is her brother Moses. Deborah is an army general on the front lines of the Hebrew people, and her brother Barak is afraid to go into battle without her. Mary is the first disciple, and far from being a shrinking virgin, she is in the upper room when the resurrected Christ appears. She becomes one of the earliest apostles of scripture. How refreshing it is to see the Bible through the eyes of strong women!

The retreat leader said something which unsettled me. She suggested that as strong women leaders in the church, we had to stop calling Jesus "Lord." A lord means that there has to be a servant and we, as women in the church, had borne the brunt of servanthood far too long. Jesus could be our friend and our teacher, but he could not be our Lord or our Savior. According to this feminist scholar, submitting to any male could no longer be the call for women created in the image of a non-gendered God.

I immediately began to argue with this leader — separating myself from the other women on the retreat. I am not a submissive person by nature and my marriage is as egalitarian as we can possibly make it. But Jesus is different. I implicitly trust Jesus to love me unconditionally and empower me whole-heartedly. His authority of truth, grace, and love is utterly dependable. It is the only dependable authority for living that I know. In company with the millions of Christians who have honored the lordship of Christ during the past 2,000 years, I willingly and lovingly submit my life and my heart to Jesus. Why? Because I trust his love. I trust his wisdom. I trust his authority. I trust that as Lord of my life, he will never lord it over me but instead, empower me to be a free and joyful servant in his name.

Friends, who are the strangers, the foreigners, the seekers in your life that can teach you something about faith?

Who can teach you something about trust in the authority of Jesus? Who can lead you to a fresh love for Jesus as Lord? What needs to change so that you can take a leap of faith — trusting that which you don't understand, listening to the "yes" of your heart instead of the "maybe" of your mind? And what will it take for you to submit yourself joyfully and completely to the authority of Jesus in your life?

The centurion teaches us the first step. Keeping our eyes on Jesus, let us offer these words: "Only speak the word, Lord, and your servant will be healed."

May it be so for you and for me. Amen.

Transfiguration of Our Lord
Luke 9:28-36 (37-43)

Now about eight days after these sayings Jesus took with him Peter and John and James, and went up on the mountain to pray. And while he was praying, the appearance of his face changed, and his clothes became dazzling white. Suddenly they saw two men, Moses and Elijah, talking to him. They appeared in glory and were speaking of his departure, which he was about to accomplish at Jerusalem. Now Peter and his companions were weighed down with sleep; but since they had stayed awake, they saw his glory and the two men who stood with him. Just as they were leaving him, Peter said to Jesus, "Master, it is good for us to be here; let us make three dwellings, one for you, one for Moses, and one for Elijah" — not knowing what he said. While he was saying this, a cloud came and overshadowed them; and they were terrified as they entered the cloud. Then from the cloud came a voice that said, "This is my Son, my Chosen; listen to him!" When the voice had spoken, Jesus was found alone. And they kept silent and in those days told no one any of the things they had seen.

Transfiguration of Our Lord
Luke 9:28-36 (37-43)

The Natural Look

It was a special day, a spiritual day, the passage from childhood into young adulthood. I was just shy of my thirteenth birthday and I was excited. For six months we had sat through boring classes memorizing the catechism, taking notes, trying to be good at God. After all, the closest thing I knew to God was my teacher, who happened to be my daddy. And I didn't want to disappoint either God or Daddy! Yes, back then confirmation was a big deal. Nobody ever dreamed of missing a class. We memorized all 196 questions in the Shorter Catechism. And we were not allowed to take communion until we were officially confirmed.

The week before the Maundy Thursday Confirmation Service, my mom and I went shopping. She bought me my first pair of stockings, my first pair of heels, and yes, my very first (and I believe last) girdle. Right before we left for church, she handed me two more small packages. In one was a perfect gold cross accompanied by tiny pearl earrings. But the other package was the most grown up gift of all. There, nestled in cotton, was my first tube of lipstick and an elegant ivory compact filled with pressed powder. Yes, indeed, if I was going to be an adult, I had to do adult things. Powdering my nose and removing the childish glow from my face seemed to be the first place to begin.

In retrospect, the message of those early sixties rituals seems bizarre. Why was it that in order to be a grownup in the church or in the world I had to be sucked in, propped up, coiffured, powdered, and adorned, replacing the natural look with the powdered look? At a moment that is meant to invite intimacy with God, I was instead donning layers of adult pretense in order to play adult games. I think that if I had it to do all over again, I would much rather bask in the natural glow of Moses than mimic the made-up machinations of Barbie.

If there was such a thing as an Oscar for the best actor in scripture, Moses would be at the top of my list. But when I imagine Moses, Charlton Heston is the last person I see. My Moses is a bit like Lou Grant — you know Mary's boss in the old *Mary Tyler Moore Show*. In my mind's eye, Moses is paunchy, bossy, bald, irreverent but he is also honest and real to the core.

By the time we meet Moses in this morning's scripture passage he has been through the mill. A stuttering shepherd and an ex-murderer, he has been commandeered by God, sputtering from the bowels of a burning bush. Tossed into the maelstrom of God's crazy plan of salvation, Moses ends up confronting Pharaoh. Then he survives nine plagues — flies and pus and boils, frogs and blood and locusts — only to lead a ragtag band of slaves through a temperamental sea into the desolation of a bitter desert. But what comes next makes the pus, the flies, and the burning heat seem delicious. There in the barren sand, all those people turn into beasts — whiny, bitter, stiff-necked children — who blame Moses for the misery and the despair of their unfinished lives.

Moses, it turns out, is no prince himself. He mumbles when he should be eloquent. He whines and complains about all his whining and complaining people. He regularly feels terrified. And when he does not feel terrified, he seethes with anger. Through it all, he carries on a verbal tug-of-war with this jerk named God who somehow dragged him into this mess to begin with. And yet, these two — Moses and God — turn out to be quite a team. Together they nourish the people, feeding them with manna, quail, and water springing from a rock. They take turns getting angry and then calming each other down while the people play their tiresome people games. Finally, God and Moses manage to get some rules written down on a stone tablet only to have them destroyed when Moses flings them aside in a fit of anger. You see, when Moses comes down from the mountain eagerly hugging the Ten Commandments to his breast, what he finds is a drunken orgy. His faithless followers are worshiping a golden calf and honoring that which is material and immediate. They are forsaking that which is mysterious and holy. Yahweh is even madder than Moses and immediately threatens to destroy *all* these sorry sinners. But wait a minute! If God destroys the people, that means God destroys Moses! The greatest stutterer of all time suddenly becomes eloquent. Moses pleads with God to save, not destroy, the people. Lo and behold, God listens! Yes, Moses manages to change God's mind! The journey continues — the journey of God's people stumbling along, but with God's fresh blessing, trying to become God's holy presence in an unholy world.

All of this is the background for today's epic scene. Through all of this turmoil and trouble, all of this toil and turbulence, Moses has grown weary and worn. He is balder, lamer, wider through the middle. But he has also grown wiser, more comfortable, more familiar, and more intimate with God. Yes, as companions traveling together through the travail of God's people, Moses and God have become friends. They have spent a lot of time together, talking things over. And though God always remains the "holy other," God is, nonetheless, available and generous, changing Moses more and more into the person he was created to be. Indeed, such intimate companionship with God has polished Moses with a particular patina of the holiness of God — the glowing image of God shining out of the very heart of who Moses is.

The text tells us that when Moses comes down from the mountain the second time, clutching version two of the Ten Commandments, his face literally shines. Why? *Because he has been talking to God.* But — and this is important — Moses does not know it. You see, far from pretense, far from politically motivated posturing, Moses is just being his fresh and real self. That means his God-drenched self, his shining self, and his authentic self. Yes, by talking with God again and again and again — by arguing, debating, asking, listening, pleading, begging, praying, and learning — Moses has slowly, over the years, become transformed — yes even transfigured. He has been changed from who the world *says* he should be — into who God has uniquely created him to be. And this completely authentic and utterly unique Moses literally shines.

Early in my career I attended a weeklong young pastor's seminar, designed to keep restless pastors from bolting from the ministry. Those who created the event knew that after five or six years of stumbling through parish ministry most of us would have had our eyes opened. Far from the ethereal vision of pious pastoring that we clung to in seminary, what we all had discovered was reality. What ministry is really about is whiny, needy pastors serving whiny, needy people and in the wilderness of all this humanness there can be the impetuous urge to desert the desert. That is why the young pastor's seminar was created. After an intense few days of discussion, worship, and study sessions, the leaders invited us to share one final exercise. Each of us sat in the middle of the group, and for ten minutes heard words to describe who we were — what the group had perceived were our strengths, as well as our weaknesses. It was absolutely awful. For ten minutes I heard someone described that had no connection with the person I know myself to be. Not only was the Susan Andrews they described a total stranger to me, I didn't even like her!

That was the day, after hours of private tears, that I decided that all the masks and all the pretense, all the *shoulds* and all the *oughts*, all the pleasing other people at the expense of pleasing God — all of it had to go. Why? Because the person I was created to be, the person I can be, the person I need and want to be, was, at that point, buried beneath deep layers of fear and obligation and control. I realize that the person I really am — the person I am still struggling to become — is sometimes hard to take — for me as well as for others. But I have also learned that unless I am authentically myself — a self created to be unique in the image of God — I cannot serve God or God's people the way only I am meant to serve them.

Today's story is about intimacy and it is about authenticity. Moses' face begins to shine and continues to shine when he finally submits to God. When he finally submits to God's intimate, insistent, gracious, pervasive presence in his life, he shines. And the more he talks to God, the more he interfaces with God, the more he engages God, the more he struggles with God, the more real Moses becomes. The more authentic Moses becomes, the more *Moses*, Moses became. And so it is with us. In an old Hasidic tale, Rabbi Zuysa says, "In the coming world, they will not ask me: 'Why were you not Moses?' They will ask me: 'Why were you not Zuysa?'"

Several generations after Moses, we find another man on a mountaintop talking fervently, intimately, comfortably with God. And his face too is shining. But it is not just his face. It is his whole body, his clothing, his entire being, glowing with the power of God. The transfiguration of Jesus happens just as Jesus is about to turn his face toward Jerusalem, toward Calvary, toward the crush of the cross and the terror of the tomb. Seeking his unique place in the creative work of God, Jesus receives stunning confirmation of who he really is. Out of the cosmos a voice echoes the original blessing of baptism: "This is my Son, my Beloved. Listen to him." And in the mystery of that holy/human moment, God becomes permanently, and irrevocably, grounded in our humanity.

My friends, as we now travel with Jesus off the mountaintop, back into the wilderness of Lent, may we cling intimately to God and to one another. And scrubbing all the pretense from our lives, may we shine with the natural and abundant grace of God.

May it be so for you and for me. Amen.

www.ingramcontent.com/pod-product-compliance
Lightning Source LLC
Chambersburg PA
CBHW071719090426
42738CB00009B/1821